811

By Professor Raymond

The Aztec God and Other Dramas . . . $1.25

" As fine lines as are to be found anywhere in English . . Sublime thought fairly leaps in sublime expression . . . as remarkable for its force of epigram as for its loftiness of conception."—*Cleveland World.*

" The plot is exceedingly interesting and well executed . . . careful work, strong and thoughtful in its conception."—*Worcester Spy.*

A Life in Song $1.25

" He has the true fire—there is no disputing that. There is thought of an elevated character, the diction is pure, the versification is true, and . . . affords innumerable quotations to fortify and instruct one for the struggles of life."—*Hartford Post.*

" . . . The versification throughout is graceful and thoroughly artistic, the imagery varied ann spontaneous . . . the multitude of contemporary bardlings may find in its sincerity of purpose and loftiness of aim a salutary inspiration."—*The Literary World* (Boston).

Ballads and Other Poems. 16°, cloth extra, gilt top $1.25

" Notable examples . . . wrought of native material by one who has a tasteful ear and practised hand. . . . There is true enjoyment in all that he has written."—*Boston Globe.*

" A work of true genius, brimful of imagination and sweet humanity." —*The Fireside* (London).

" Fine and strong, its thought original and suggestive, while its expression is the very perfection of narrative style."—*The N. Y. Critic.*

" The work of a genuine poet."—*N. Y. Evening Post.*

Poetry as a Representative Art. 8° . . $1.75

" I have read it with pleasure and a sense of instruction on many points."—*Francis Turner Palgrave, Professor of Poetry, Oxford University.*

"Dieses ganz vortreffliche Werk."—*Englische Studien, Universität Breslau.*

Rhythm and Harmony in Poetry and Music. 8° $1.75

" The reader must be, indeed, a person either of supernatural stupidity or of marvellous erudition, who does not discover much information in Prof. Raymond's exhaustive and instructive treatise. From page to page it is full of suggestion."—*The Academy* (London).

Art in Theory ($1.75), The Representative Significance of Form ($2.00), Painting, Sculpture, and Architecture, as Representative Arts ($2.50), The Genesis of Art-Form ($2.25), Proportion and Harmony of Line and Color in Painting, Sculpture, and Architecture ($2.50) and a compendium of the others, The Essentials of Æsthetics ($2.50).

" The whole philosophy underlying this intelligent art-criticism . . . should be given the widest possible publicity."—*Boston Globe.*

" One of the best systems of art criticism and interpretation in the English tongue."—*N. Y. Mail and Express.*

DANTE

AND

COLLECTED VERSE

BY

GEORGE LANSING RAYMOND

G. P. PUTNAM'S SONS

NEW YORK AND LONDON

The Knickerbocker Press

1909

21272

The Knickerbocker Press, New York

CONTENTS.

DANTE.

PAGE

DANTE 5

NOTES UPON DANTE 127

MOUNTAINS ABOUT WILLIAMSTOWN.

GREYLOCK 145

BERLIN MOUNTAIN 150

WEST MOUNTAIN 157

PARALLELS AND PARABLES.

THE LAST HOME-GATHERING . . . 171

MIDNIGHT IN A CITY PARK . . . 178

IDEALS THAT WERE 183

THE SAILOR'S CHOICE 184

AT THE PARTING OF THE WAYS . . 188

THE RELIGION OF RESCUE . . . 189

AFTER THE LYNCHING 192

RIGHTING A WRONG 196

SHE WONDERS WHY 200

PAGE

The Wall-Flower 201

Homeless 202

The Blizzard 203

In the Life Beyond 204

SUGGESTIONS FROM CHURCH, STATE AND SOCIETY.

A Hymn for All Religions 209

The American Pioneer 211

God Bless America 214

To the Wife of a Public Man . . . 216

Her Haughtiness 219

The Society Leader 222

LOVE AND LIFE.

Love and Life 227

SONNETS.

The Leader 277

The Solitary Singer 277

Staking All 278

Obscurity 279

Influence 280

The Final Verdict 281

PAGE

THE CHANCE THAT COMES TO EVERY MAN . 281
HEREDITY 282
UNCONSCIOUS CHARM 283
IN THE ART MUSEUM 284
THE CLIMBER 284
SENSE AND SOUL 285
CLASS AND CASTE 286
THE FAITH THAT DOUBTS 287
BROADENING THE OUTLOOK 287
OUR AFFINITY 288
MY ACTRESS 289
THE FIRST FASCINATION 290
THE LOST FRIEND 290
FOR A BOOK MADE UP OF CONTRIBUTIONS FROM
    AUTHORS 291
FORD'S GLEN, WILLIAMSTOWN 292
PRINCETON UNIVERSITY 293
PRINCETON CEMETERY 294
BONAVENTURE CEMETERY, SAVANNAH . . 294
THE GRAVE OF GENIUS 295

SONGS AND HYMNS.

WHERE DWELL THE GODS 299
ALL HAIL THE GOD. 300
OH, NOT WHAT LIFE APPEARS TO BE . . 302

PAGE

ALL HAIL THE SUN 302

O LIFE DIVINE 303

O GOD OF ALL THINGS LIVING . . . 304

HAIL TO THE HERO HOME FROM STRIFE . . 305

O SOUL, WHAT EARTHLY CROWN . . . 306

ALL HAIL THE QUEEN 307

WE LIVE BUT FOR BUBBLES 308

OH, WHO HAS KNOWN 309

TWO SPRINGS OF LIFE 310

IN THE WORLD OF CARE AND SORROW . . 311

THE TRUMPETS CALL TO ACTION . . . 312

OH, WHY DO WE CARE 313

AH, BOYS, WHEN WE FILL OUR GLASSES . . 314

OUR LIVES ARE VAPORS 315

MONEY AND MAN 316

JUST THE THING HE THINKS . . . 317

NOT FREE TO ME 320

A FAIRY SONG 322

LOVE AND TRUTH 324

THE WORLD THAT WHIRLS FOREVER . . 325

FATHER OF OUR SPIRITS, HEAR US . . 327

DAN**TE**.

1

CHARACTERS.

DANTE (Alighieri)	The Great Italian Poet.
(Guido) CAVALCANTI	A Poet and Patron of Dante, about ten years older than he; a Leader of the White Faction.
CINO (a Pistoja)	A Poet and Friend of Dante, but somewhat younger than he; a Member of the White Faction.
DINO (Frescobaldi)	A Poet and Friend of Dante, about the same age as he; a Member of the White Faction.
(Cosmo) DONATI	The Leader of the Black Faction, and Dante's Enemy.
SIMONE (Donati)	Son of Cosmo Donati, and Dante's Enemy.
(Brunetto) LATINI	An aged Teacher of Florence, much respected by Dante and his Friends.
BEATRICE (Portina)	A Young Maiden, greatly beloved by Dante.
GEMMA (Donati)	A Young Maiden, Niece of Cosmo Donati, who became Dante's Wife.
BACCHINA	A Young Maiden, a companion of Beatrice and Gemma.

3

MARQUIS OF MALASPINA in Lunigiana, a Protector of
Dante in exile.

WAITRESS, PRIEST, MONK, MESSENGERS, ATTENDANTS,
CHAPERON, YOUNG MEN, MAIDENS, AND ADHERENTS
of the White and Black Factions.

Place and Time, Florence and Italy in the Fourteenth
Century.

All the men in the play who are not ecclesiastics
wear belts from which hang scabbards holding swords.

———

A poet like a poem is a product.
DANTE, I. AND VI.

All the thoughts
That flood the world spring up from single souls;
And some of these may bless it most when made
To spend their lives interpreting themselves.
IDEM II.

DANTE.

OPENING TABLEAU.

*The Piazza di Santa Croce in Florence, Italy.
Backing is the Church of Santa Croce. In front
of it are the beginnings of a Pedestal. On the
highest part of this, accompanied by others below
her, with whom she is playing, is a young girl
(BEATRICE) dressed in a dark crimson frock.
Below, on the pavement gazing at her, stands a
schoolboy (DANTE), who seems to have been
suddenly arrested and charmed by her appearance.*[1]

ACT FIRST.

SCENE:—*The Piazza di Santa Croce in Florence,
arranged for a Fête, as on St. John's Day,
when, to quote from Federn's Dante, "the
young men, clad in white, led by the Signor
d'Amour, went singing and dancing up the
street of Santa Felicita; and women and girls,
. . . in wreaths of flowers, partook in the fes-
tivities; and music and song and ringing bells*

*filled the air with joyful sounds." Backing at
the Right, is a bench, at the Left, half-way to the
Front, is a booth arranged for the fête. In it
is a table on which are flowers, apparently for
sale, also at least one bottle of wine and three
glasses. Entrances at the Right Front and
Upper, and at the Left Front and Upper. The
Curtain, as it rises, reveals, at the Back Center,
the aged Teacher* LATINI, *surrounded by three
young men,—*CAVALCANTI, *about thirty years
of age, and* CINO *and* DINO, *about twenty. The
three hold in their hands pencils and manuscripts which can be easily carried in their
pockets.*[2] *Behind the table, stands a matron
serving as a Waitress in the fête.*

LATINI. A poet like a poem is a product.
CINO. I thought him born, not made.
LATINI.   And why not both?
  Let nature frame a man to feel. He thinks
  Of what he feels. He feels what touches him.
  The substance of his thought and feeling then
  Is what experience has brought near to him.
CINO. But men term youth poetic.
LATINI.   Rightly too.
  The freshest fires are brightest. But our
    thoughts,

How e'er they burn and melt, not often flow
To moulds of nature's rarest imagery,
Till life has been well sought to find and store
    it.

CINO.   Then youth should wait for age, and grow
    apace,
And try no more.

LATINI.   O no; it is our trying
That turns the latch-key of experience,
Whose doors swing inward quite as oft as
    outward.

    Enter—Left Upper—Several Pairs of danc-
       ing YOUNG MEN *and* MAIDENS. *They*
       sing:

How green the grove and blue the sky!
   How gold and red the hedges!
How thrills the breeze with trills on high,
   That breathe the season's pledges!
For, O, the spring, in all its prime,
Has brought the bird its mating-time.

    *Enter—Right Upper—*DANTE.
    *Exeunt—Right Front—*DANCERS.
    *Enter—Left Upper—*GEMMA *and* BACCHINA,
       and between them BEATRICE.[3] *The*
       three walk arm in arm, and exchange

> *bows with the Gentlemen,* BEATRICE
> *taking especial notice of* DANTE.

CINO (*to* DINO, *as he looks toward the three*).
  A trinity appropriate for St. John's Day!

DINO.   The poet's graces!

CINO (*moving toward the three*).
                          And the poet's models.
  They bring us dies, when our ideas glow,
  To leave their impress and remain ideals.

> DANTE, *upon seeing* BEATRICE, *seems
> greatly embarrassed, and sits apart by
> himself on the Bench alternately writing
> in a manuscript that he holds, and listen-
> ing to the conversation of the others.*[7]

BEATRICE (*to* LATINI).   We come to tender you
  our morning greeting.

CAVALCANTI (*to* DINO).   Nor could the tender
  come more tenderly.

LATINI (*shaking hands with the three young
  women*).   I thank you.

BACCHINA (*turning to* DINO).   Will you recom-
  mend me now?

DINO.   For what?

BACCHINA.   Why, if a king's touch cure
  king's evil,
  A master's touch should cure the master's evil.

DINO.   And what is that?

Bacchina (*looking toward* Latini).   All evil in
    the world,
  To him, is lack of culture.
Dino.   So you seek
  To come in touch with him?
Bacchina (*laughingly*).   And with his pupils.
(*Giving her hand to* Dino. *Both join in the
        dance that follows.*)
Enter—Right Upper—Pairs of Dancing Young
    Men *and* Maidens. *They Sing:*

> How keen the glance, and bright the flush!
>   How sense the soul resembles!
> How throbs the heart that heed would hush
>   Through lips where music trembles!
> For, O, the spring of round and rhyme
> Has brought mankind its mating-time!

*   Exeunt—Left Front—*Dancers.
*   Enter—Left Upper—*Donati.
Cino *and* Dino *talk with* Gemma *and* Bacchina.
Cavalcanti (*to* Beatrice).   You heard what
    Cino said.   It all was true.
  The hands of beauty when they touch and
    thrill us
  All leave their imprint on ideas, and thus
  We get ideals.
Beatrice (*laughingly*).   You poets wing your
    words

Without the least conception where they wend,
Like birds with broken feet that keep on
    flying
From simple inability to perch.

DONATI.   Ha, ha!

CAVALCANTI (*to* DONATI).   You heard her then?

DONATI.   I overheard.

CAVALCANTI (*aside to* DINO).

Is always overing something, if he can be.

DONATI (*to* BEATRICE).   Well said, Miss Be-
    atrice!   These flighty minds
That cut connection with the world's demands
Are sure to have a limping time of it,
If ever they get down to useful work.

> (BEATRICE *laughs and bows, then with*
>   CINO *joins* GEMMA *and* BACCHINA *at
>   the Left where all seem to be helping the
>   Matron who has charge of the Table.*
>   DINO *sits on the Bench beside* DANTE.
>   *They exchange, and, apparently, in a
>   friendly way, criticise each other's
>   writings*).[4]

CAVALCANTI (*replying to* DONATI'S *last remark*).

They may prove useful without getting down
    As far as—[5]

DONATI.   Useful as the splash and spray
Above the waterfall that works my mill.

CAVALCANTI. They play a necessary part.

DONATI. You own
They play?

CAVALCANTI. And play is necessary too.
Our thoughts are children that must play to
grow.

DONATI. Say children that when called to work
must whine.
These brains that bellow so about their pains,
Prove mainly their own lack of brawn to bear
them.

CAVALCANTI. At least, they lead a peaceful life,
not so?—
And that is better than a life of brawls.

DONATI. Who lead a life of brawls?

CAVALCANTI. I did not say;
But many a night in Florence is termed black.

DONATI. And many a coward's face is well
termed white.

CAVALCANTI (*drawing his sword, which* DONATI
also does).
Now by my sword!

CINO. Nay, nay; but by your sense.
What fevers both of you is no disease
That can be cured by surgery.

CAVALCANTI. By what then?

CINO (*pointing to the table, and rapidly filling
three glasses from the bottle*).
By stimulants.   Accurse to cutting down,
When one can gulp down! Save your health
for me,
And, while you sheathe your swords, pledge
gratitude
For such delicious ways of sheathing spirits.
(DONATI *and* CAVALCANTI *sheathe their swords
and drink with* CINO.)
> *Exeunt—Left Upper—*CAVALCANTI, DON-
> ATI, *and* CINO *with glasses in hand, fol-
> lowed by the Waitress carrying the bottle.*
(DINO, *when he sees them, excusing himself to*
DANTE, *rises and follows them.*)
> *Exit—Left Upper—*DINO.
GEMMA (*to* BEATRICE, *looking toward the Left*).
Ha, ha!
BEATRICE.   What set you laughing?
GEMMA.   Why, to think
My uncle's words could turn a poet's thought
Out of his own conceit—humph!—long enough
To take in the conception of another.
BEATRICE.   You like not poets then?
BACCHINA.   They like not her.
GEMMA.   They might, if they could see me.
What they see

Is never in the thing at which they look;
But, like a halo when it rings the moon,
All in the clouds, and drawn there by them-
    selves.

BEATRICE.   Break through the halo, you might
    find them out.

BACCHINA.   Or else be found out by them.

GEMMA.   That is it;
    And by-and-by come tumbling from the
      hights
    Where they, not we, have put us,—in a realm
    Where pebbles all seem palaces, and mounds
      all mounts,
    And clouds all continents, and moons have
      faces,
    And all the littlest stars that prick the sky
    Are spear-points of some huge hobgoblin.

BEATRICE.   To think things larger may enlarge
    one's thought.

GEMMA.   To think things true when false may
    prove all false.

BEATRICE.   Who think the poets' fancies true?
    Their brains,
    Like helmets when their metal is the best,
    Receive the light of life and flash it back.
    None take the flash for fire.

GEMMA.   I see you like
  A fancy, flashing fellow!—I the grave
  And thoughtful.

BEATRICE.   Fancy is the flower of thought.
  The more of life there is, the more of flower:
  The more of thought there is, the more of
    fancy.
  A bear, you know, has hair upon his cheek,
  And growls, and, now and then, stands up and
    hugs.
  I like men who can prove themselves no brutes.
      (DANTE *sits staring at* BEATRICE.)
        *Enter—Left Upper—*DONATI.

DONATI (*noticing* DANTE *and addressing him*).
  Why, Dante, you here? [6]

DANTE (*rising in embarrassment*).   Yes.

DONATI (*shaking hands with* DANTE).   Good
  day.

GEMMA (*aside to* BEATRICE *and* BACCHINA).
  His "yes"
  Outsnubs the backset of a tutor's "no,"—
  Forbids all further effort at expression.

DONATI (*to* DANTE *and gesturing toward the*
  YOUNG WOMEN).
  You know these ladies, do you not?

DANTE (*bowing awkwardly*).   Yes, yes. [7]

DONATI. What writing is it that you hold in
hand?

(DANTE *closes his manuscript, and puts it inside
his cloak.*)

A secret?

DANTE (*bowing awkwardly*). Yes.

> *Exit—Left Upper—*DONATI, *laughing.*
> *Enter—Right Upper—*CINO.

(CINO *and* DANTE *sit on the Bench and exchange
writings.*[4])

GEMMA (*to* YOUNG WOMEN *at the Left, and referring to* DANTE'S *manuscript.*)

His own child, probably!
It flies to cover so much like himself.
He is a very interesting man.

BEATRICE. You think so?

GEMMA. To himself. When all
one's eyes
And ears are turned like his on his own person,
He bears about both audience and actor.

Enter—Left Upper—Several Pairs of Dancing
YOUNG MEN *and* MAIDENS. *They sing:*

> How framed in grace and phrased in song,
>   How homed in rapture real,
> How won to worth from earth and wrong
>   Is love when once ideal!

For, O, the spring of life sublime
Has brought the spirit's mating-time!

*Exeunt—Right Front—*DANCERS.
*Enter—Left Front—*CAVALCANTI.

CAVALCANTI (*to* BEATRICE). My gentle maid,
  Miss Beatrice, not dancing?

BEATRICE.   Not now, rough master Cavalcanti.

CAVALCANTI.   Oh!

BEATRICE.   Oh?—We must speak as we are
  spoken to;
  And if I be a maid and gentle also
  You ought to be my master and be rough.

CAVALCANTI.   Be rough?—Oh, never. I leave
  that to Dante.

BEATRICE.   I should think so!

CAVALCANTI.   Wait, Miss Beatrice.
  A man may double up his fist and frown,
  And make fiend-faces merely at himself.

BEATRICE.   Why so?

CAVALCANTI.   Because that self asserts itself;
  And he keeps fighting it to keep it down.

BEATRICE.   That self must then be very strong.

CAVALCANTI.   It is—
  In Dante.

BEATRICE.   Humph!—Is that what troubles
  him?

*Enter—Right Upper—*DINO.

CINO *rises, leaves* DANTE, *and goes to meet*
DINO, *where standing at the Right they*
also seem to criticise each other's
manuscripts.[4]

CAVALCANTI. It is with you. You have such
awful eyes.
They hush him so his inward soul stops think-
ing;
And then his outward mien plays pedagogue
And whips himself to make himself behave.

BEATRICE. A very strange man!

CAVALCANTI. You should not say that.
Just think how hot he must be in his heart
To make him warp and shrink up as he
does
When you come near.

BEATRICE. He does not act that way
With others?

CAVALCANTI. No.

BEATRICE. Some people act that way
With cats. Kind souls then shoo these off.

BEATRICE *joins* GEMMA *and* BACCHINA, *and,*
presently,

*Exeunt—Left Front—*GEMMA, BEATRICE, *and*
BACCHINA.

2

DINO (*looking at the* YOUNG WOMEN, *to* CINO).
    A poet has to pose, to prose himself
    Sufficiently for some companionship.
CINO.   To one who wed her, she would prove
        to be
    A pretty but a pert Lupatto-dog,
    And snarl at all who did not master her.
DINO (*looking sharply at* DANTE).
    But why does Dante gaze at Gemma so?
    Finds her inspiring?—I would rather risk,
    Without a disenchanting yell or yolp,
    Extracting teeth than thought from such a
        mouth.
    *Exeunt—Right Front—*CINO *and* DINO.
DANTE (*rising and speaking to* CAVALCANTI,
    who has approached him).
    Say, Cavalcanti, did you hear those words?—
    "Why does he gaze at Gemma?"—did you
        hear?
    Say, Cavalcanti, did you hear?—"at Gemma"?
    They must imagine—[8]
CAVALCANTI.   Yes, they must imagine.
    They never could have seen it with their eyes.
DANTE.   Seen what?
CAVALCANTI.   Now, Dante, I have made no
    claim
    To be your soul's confessor; but you know

That I have guessed to whom you wrote your
    verses;
And you have not denied it.—Was it Gemma?

DANTE. The next time that men watch me,
    they shall think so.[8]

CAVALCANTI. And why?

DANTE. No doubt, no thought! What men
    conceive
They comprehend, they cease to guess about.

CAVALCANTI. Would you deceive them?

DANTE.   What men have no right
To know, one has no right to let them know.
Because my soulless will has made me brute,
And kept me staring like a pointer-cur
As if to turn to prey the very one
I most revere, must then my voice, forsooth,
Bark out an insult in the same direction?

CAVALCANTI. I did not say that, boy; but it
    were strange
To see you start to play the very game
That you blame me for.

DANTE.   Nay, I should not say
My love sought more than one.

CAVALCANTI.   Nor I, you know—
Were it not true.

DANTE.   Oh, fickle Cavalcanti!

CAVALCANTI.　Your humming bees may sip the
　　sweets they need

　From every flower; and why not humming
　　poets?

DANTE.　They were not made to sting, nor
　　souls for stinging.

　The poets are not lesser men but greater;

　And so should find unworthy of themselves

　A word or deed that makes them seem less
　　worthy.

　A man should court but one, and marry
　　her.

CAVALCANTI.　And mar the lives of all he does
　　not marry?

DANTE.　Nay, nay; be true to one, and let the
　　church—

CAVALCANTI.　The church can but confirm a
　　fact that is,—[9]

　A love that lives already in the soul.

　Not outside hands, though reaching down
　　from heaven,

　Can push inside of it what is not there,

　Nor keep aught inside, would it then pass
　　out.

　You deem it wise or good, humane or Godly,

　To doom a boy for one mistake in mating

　To everlasting punishment on earth?

*Enter—Left Front—*Gemma.

  Ah, Mistress Gemma, Master Dante here
Was looking at you, so that I rebuked him.
Gemma. Was looking—and at what?
Cavalcanti.   Why, I should say
Your ribbons—things that he could tie to.
Dante.   Oh!
Cavalcanti. But that was what we just were
    talking of,—
  A something on the earth, and it wears ribbons,
  That one can tie to.
Gemma.   Making free, I think,
  With my own ribbons!
Cavalcanti.   No, no; making them
  So they would not be free.
Gemma.   Yes, they might choke me.
Dante. And what a pity that would be!
Gemma.   Why so?
Dante. These choking throats make faces red.
Gemma.   Make red?
Dante. Yes; yours I never yet saw *read*. It
    seemed
  A readless riddle.
Gemma.   It could riddle you.
Dante. Oh, no; you would not judge enough
    was in me
  To justify the jog. Why tap a void?

*Enter—Right Front—*BEATRICE.

> CAVALCANTI *goes to her.* DANTE, *standing at the Left with his back to the Right, does not see her.*

GEMMA (*to* DANTE). You may be right,—more right than you suppose.

DANTE. More right than I suppose?—It is not often

One does me so much honor.

> (*They continue talking at the Left.*)

BEATRICE (*to* CAVALCANTI, *while she stands at the Right looking at* DANTE).

Yes, I read
The song you say that Dante wrote about me.
But were he truthful, did he feel it all,
It were but natural for him to speak
To me.

CAVALCANTI. He is an artist.

BEATRICE. What of that?

CAVALCANTI. You know there were no art, were there no forms

Of nature in which art could frame its tribute.
But many an artist, for this reason, fears
To emphasize the part he finds in nature
Lest it outdo the part he finds in self;
So often that which seems most natural
The one thing is that he will not let seem so.

BEATRICE (*looking toward* GEMMA).

How smitten he is with her! [18]

CAVALCANTI. Whom—with Gemma?

BEATRICE. Of course.

CAVALCANTI. You think so?

BEATRICE. See him hold
her hand.

CAVALCANTI. If your hand were where hers is,
I believe

His own would tremble so he could but drop
it.

GEMMA (*to* DANTE, *while he takes her hand as if
to bid good-bye*).

But had I no imagination?

DANTE. Then,
I could not see my image in you, could I?
And if—to quote you—I but think of self,
You could not make me think of anything.

GEMMA. I could not help you much then?
*Exit—Right Front—*BEATRICE.

DANTE. No; not if
Myself be what I think.

(GEMMA *and* DANTE *bow to each other.*)
*Exit—Left Front—*GEMMA.

(DANTE *takes his manuscript from his pocket, and
begins to write.*)

CAVALCANTI (*approaching, and laying his hand
    on* DANTE'S *shoulder*).

                    What are you doing?

DANTE.   Am writing.

CAVALCANTI.   Yes, I saw that.—Writing
    what?

DANTE.   What comes to me. [10]

CAVALCANTI (*with a gesture toward the Left
    Front*).

                        From her?

DANTE.   Yes, partly
    so; And partly from myself.

CAVALCANTI.   You write it down
    To save it?

DANTE.   Yes, and save myself.   You know
    That writing is my mission. [10]

CAVALCANTI.   What was that
    Which she suggested?

DANTE (*after hesitating a moment*).   Why some
    minds that try

To be in touch with ours but tickle them;

Or vex an itching that can merely fret us.

Withal, too, they but scratch the brain's out-
    side;

And then, as if they took the hair for thought,

Exhibit this, when tossed and puffed, as prov-
    ing

How they themselves have thus our brain de-
veloped.

CAVALCANTI (*laughing heartily, then taking from
his pocket a manuscript poem*).

No touch like that, though, led you to write
this, [11]

Why is it, boy, you hold your love so secret?

DANTE. Had you a glimpse of God like no one
else's

You would not speak of it?

CAVALCANTI.   Why not?

DANTE.   It might

Subject Him to the insult—might it not?—
Of human doubt?

CAVALCANTI.   You are a strange soul, Dante.

DANTE. You think my verses good?

CAVALCANTI.   Both good and bad.

DANTE. Why bad?

CAVALCANTI.   Oh, not so fierce! Not you are
bad;

And not your verses when they come from you.

DANTE. From whom else could they come?

CAVALCANTI.   I seem to hear

The echoes through them of your masters.

DANTE.   Good ones!

CAVALCANTI. Good masters give us methods
but not models.

You write as one who rests in a ravine
Recording but what others have beheld
Above where he dare venture.

DANTE.   You would have me?—

CAVALCANTI.   Climb up, or soar—

DANTE.   But how?

CAVALCANTI.   The spirit's wings
Are grown, not given, unfold within oneself.
But you—you get both word and thought
    from others.

DANTE.   You mean my Latin?

CAVALCANTI.   Yes, I mean your Latin. [1][2]

DANTE.   The words of Virgil and the Christian
    Church,—
The thoughts that live like spirits in the
    words,
And save our own thought through what they
    incarnate!

CAVALCANTI. The thought they save should
    be your own, my Dante.
Are you a Roman?   You should be Italian [1][2]
With theme and language fitted for Italians.
To lift the lives of common men, it is,
That poems make the common seem uncom-
    mon,
Their richest boon, believe me, that which
    brings

To him who reads an inward consciousness
Of oneness with the spirit that indites them,
And its own oneness with the loftiest spirit.

DANTE. The poet's tool is his poetic tongue.

CAVALCANTI. 'T is not the tongue that makes
   the bell ring sweet;

It is the metal of the bell itself.

   *Enter—Right Front—*MESSENGER.

   (*to* MESSENGER.)

Good day.   You seem excited.

MESSENGER.   Yes, I am.

Will never fate decree a time of rest
For Florence?

CAVALCANTI. Not while wide awake!   What
   now?

MESSENGER.   A courier has just come speeding
   in.

He says the Ghibellines take arms again,[13]
Have fresh recruits enlisted at Arezzo,
Have fortified the castle at Caprona,
And gather now in force at Campaldino.

DANTE.   And we do nothing?

MESSENGER.   Yes, Donati's Blacks

Like flocks of feeding crows we pelt with peb-
   bles

Are flying all to saddle.

DANTE.   We should follow.

CAVALCANTI.　　And follow him?—no, no.[5]

DANTE.　　　　　　　　　　Not follow him?—
Not that great fighter?

CAVALCANTI.　　　　　　　What?—you call him
great?—
Mere bluffer of some baby brawls in Florence?
The flimsiest nerve can fret to feel a flea.

DANTE.　　But those who fight when no one needs
to fight—

CAVALCANTI.　　Are foes to public order.[16]　Why,
you seem
To deem all people patriots like yourself.
A little rill just starting from a spring
Could not be quite so gushing fresh as you are!
I love you, boy; but when the rill has rubbed
A little more of soil from both its banks
'T will have more substance if not quite
So much transparency.

*Enter—Left Upper—*BEATRICE, GEMMA, *and*
BACCHINA.

Unseen by DANTE, *they busy themselves with
the flowers on the table.*

DANTE.　　　　　　　　　Yet, Cavalcanti,
There is but one thing now for us to do.
Do two things, and we do the thing they
plan,—

To fight both Black and White, and each time
   half
Our full defence. Now who remembers faction
Forgets his Florence.

CAVALCANTI.   True!—and you would
   fight?

DANTE. For right to serve the Church and
   Italy?—
Fight those whose flags all fly to signal
   traitors?—
Fight those who all, like base train-bearers,
   come
To smother down the freedom of the city
Beneath an emperor's cloak whose utmost
   edge
Is fringed with bleeding spears?—Were I a
   moth
In a rug their crowd came trampling, I should
   fight—
Ay, with my mouth, too, as you seem to ask—
And keep on fighting there, until I wrought
My way to something that could not be tram-
   pled.

CAVALCANTI. All right, boy, you shall have
   your chance. We go.

*Exeunt—Right Front—*CAVALCANTI, DANTE, *and*
MESSENGER.

*Enter—Left Front—*LATINI, CINO, *and* DINO.

BEATRICE (*referring to* DANTE'S *words that all have evidently overheard*).

And that is Dante!

BEATRICE, GEMMA, *and* BACCHINA *come toward the Left Front.*

LATINI.   Yes, the actual Dante.

BEATRICE.   His words and ways have seemed so void of grace,
To say not grit!

LATINI.   In temperaments like his
The form is but the signal of the spirit.
We never judge a flag by gawky flops
Against a wind-forsaken pole; but by
Its flying when it feels the breath of heaven.

BEATRICE.   He seemed a woman; now he seems all man.

LATINI.   And both are fit in one ordained to be
A representative of all things human.
If he by nature be a poet, then
He should by nature be in substance that
Which art demands of him in semblance.

DINO.   Cino,
We should go home.

CINO.   What for?

DINO.   To put on kilts,
And show ourselves half women.

LATINI. Nay, without that,
My Dino, you can prove your womanhood;
For who but women take all words to heart,
And think each point we make must point
toward them?

*Exeunt—Right Front—*LATINI, CINO, *and* DINO.

GEMMA. He may be right; but men half done,
like eggs
Half boiled, are very soft. I much prefer
To have them hard.

BACCHINA. How strange!

GEMMA. Why strange?

BACCHINA. Because
I thought we always liked our opposites.[14]

BEATRICE. You mean?

GEMMA. Ay, you do well to call her
mean.
If when we walk, we bring our weeds with us,
We cannot hope our air to smell of roses.

BACCHINA. Aha! Humph!—That explains it!

GEMMA. What?

BACCHINA. The way
You take in breath (*tossing up her head and
nose*).

GEMMA. Look up, not down, eh?—I
Would rather snatch at birds than dig for
worms.

BACCHINA. Have pity, Gemma! Shell your
　　thoughts before
　　You fling them at us—are so hard to crack!
　　You surely would not have them crack our
　　skulls?

GEMMA. Crack moulds of jelly! Your skulls
　　were more soft
　　Than that to be indented by a Dante.

*Enter—Right Upper—*CAVALCANTI *and* DANTE.

The YOUNG WOMEN *are at the Left, and do not
notice their hearers.*

BEATRICE. A steed we drive, a stream that
　　floods its banks,
　　Has not less force because its gait is gentle.
　　And you, you heard his call a moment since
　　To Cavalcanti who behind him leads
　　The half of Florence! 'T was a call as brave
　　As ever yet were eagles', when their beaks
　　Tear out the intruder's heart, though twice
　　their size,
　　Who comes to steal the young within their
　　nests.

While BEATRICE *is speaking* DANTE *takes out his
manuscript and writes.*

*Exeunt—Left Front—*BACCHINA, GEMMA, *and*
BEATRICE.

DANTE (*to* CAVALCANTI, *referring to* BEATRICE'S
    words).

Ah, Cavalcanti, should my sword not save
The soul within me, when the strife comes on,
No welcome could await in realms beyond
So sweet, so sacred, as I just have heard![15]

CAVALCANTI.   Stay here, boy, stay!   To make a
    worthy fight,
A man should put his heart in what he does.
Your heart is lost.   It will be left behind you.

DANTE.   There, there, again, you will not under-
    stand me.

CAVALCANTI.   Now Dante!

DANTE.   Yes, you think my heart would stay
When she it is has flung it toward the fight.
What love I have, inspires me in my soul;
And, like the soul, it must express itself
Through every fibre binding me to life;
And like the soul, too, I believe it comes
From some far realm divine to make divine
Myself, my world, and all that dwell in it.
A man who feels like this, and would not fight
For church and state and home, would be a
    devil.

CAVALCANTI.   And how long, think you, in a
    world like ours,
That you can feel like this?

3

DANTE.   As long as love
   Like what I have inspires me.
CAVALCANTI.   Should it fail?
DANTE.   Then you nor anyone could longer find
   In me a friend.   All any life is worth
   Lies in its possibilities of love.
CAVALCANTI.   But were love's object lost?—
DANTE.   One cannot lose
   What is eternal.   Hearts must always keep,
   If not their love, what love has made of them.

   Enter—Left Upper—The YOUNG MEN *and*
         MAIDENS *who were the Dancers in the*
         earlier part of this Act; but the MEN *are*
         equipped for battle and walk seriously
         and the MAIDENS *follow them with every*
         indication of anxiety.   CAVALCANTI *and*
         DANTE, *the latter putting his manuscript*
         in his pocket, join them.

   *Exeunt—Right Front—*OMNES.

CURTAIN.

ACT SECOND.

SCENE: *Same as in Act First, but not arranged for a fête. The rising curtain reveals* LATINI, DINO *and other citizens of Florence, also* WOMEN.

*Enter—Right Front—*CAVALCANTI *and* CINO.

LATINI (*shaking hands with* CAVALCANTI).

And so you have returned victorious.

DINO. Thanks to Donati!

CAVALCANTI. Thanks to him I fear.

DINO Why fear it?

CAVALCANTI. One should always fear the hand
That taps a leaking jail to flood its faction. [16]
Who breaks one law may live to break another.
This very latest victory was gained
Against the orders on our side, as well
As those that they opposed upon the other.

DINO. So much the stronger he!

LATINI. Beware of strength
That, like the brute's, is wielded not by reason.
Except by reason thought was never forced
For its own good.

DINO. But if, in some just cause?—

35

LATINI. In lands where law supports the right,
    to seek
  To rise by breaking legal barriers
  Is worse than climbing up a dizzy stair
  By leaning on a broken bannister.
DINO. You may be right; but few will think
    you so.
  The man who tramples on his country's foes
  Treads upward toward a hight, however
    gained,
  Where all his countrymen look up to him.
CINO. And now but one can rival him.
LATINI.   That one?
CINO. Is Dante.
LATINI.   Dante?
CINO.   Yes, our Dante! Oh,
  You should have seen him when the battle
    came.
  He led the last charge, speeding on a steed [17]
  Well nigh as white as was the air it slid
    through,
  His form bent down as if to hurl his head
  Against their lines, and, by sheer force of
    brain,
  Burst through them. Faster than the follow-
    ing wind
  He flew, as if the blast that urged him on

Were some last trump of Gabriel's, and the
    soul
Could fear no ills, for it had passed beyond
    them.
    (*looking toward the Right Upper*)
I think him coming now.
LATINI.   He is.
DINO.   And with him
Comes Donati.
CINO.   Watching well the man
That brought him victory.
CAVALCANTI.   Too well, I fear!
You give to one who never gives to others,
He first will recognize you as a dupe,
And then prepare to treat you as a prey.
DINO. They fought for Florence.
CAVALCANTI.   Dante, not Donati.
He fights that all may follow his own standard.
*Enter—Right Upper—*DANTE, DONATI, SIMONE,
      and OTHERS *of the Blacks.*
    *Enter—Left Upper—*POPULACE.
POPULACE. Hurrah for Dante!
DANTE.   Nay, nay; say Donati.
A CITIZEN. The charge that clove their line
    for us was yours.
DANTE. Praise not the spear that split the
    foeman's mail,

But praise the brain whence came the skill
  that aimed it.

> DANTE *shakes hands with* LATINI, CINO,
>   DINO, *and* OTHERS, *then takes out his
>   manuscript and begins to write, and,
>   after a while, to talk with* CAVALCANTI
>   *at the Left Front.*

*Exeunt—Left Front—*LATINI, CINO, DINO, *and
  the* POPULACE.

SIMONE (*to* DONATI, *at extreme Right and re-
  fering to* DANTE'S *words*).
  Well said!

DONATI.　　　　It was.　That soft thing termed
  a sponge
Will always hug you, when in touch with it.
But no one finds the least impression left
When you are not in touch with it.

SIMONE.　　　　　　　　　　　I see.
  You think then that he fears you in your presence.

DONATI. I think he may not fear me in my
  absence.

SIMONE. You doubt him?

DONATI.　　　　　　　When I choose a follower,
My standard must be followed,—not his own.

He lets his own thought lead him; and you
    know
Men led by thought are often led to doubt.

SIMONE. One thinking follower might make
    men believe
Your other followers were controlled by
    thought.

DONATI (*laughingly*). You think a thug could
    ever pose as thinker?

*Enter—Right Upper—*GEMMA *and* BACCHINA *and
another* WOMAN.

GEMMA (*to* DONATI, *and looking toward* DANTE).
And is it true he led the charge?

DONATI.   They say so.
A brave man, Gemma! but, of course, you
    know it;
Has dared to press a suit with you, I hear.
          (GEMMA *nods.*)
A hero, yes! You might not go amiss—
I mean remain a Miss—had he his way.

(GEMMA *looks toward* DANTE. DONATI *continues to* SIMONE.)

If made a member of our family,
He might prove ours in all things. Few have
    brains
Too cool and clear to feel a rise in blood
And not be fevered and confused by it.

No poison paralyzes thought like pride;
No pride as poisonous as family pride.

BACCHINA (*to* GEMMA, *and looking toward*
DANTE.)

Oh, one could give a world of common men
For just one armful of a man like that!

OTHER WOMAN.   He must have trained his eyes
when he was flying.

They look as deep down through one as
an eagle's,
Ay, not as if belonging to the senses
But to the soul!

GEMMA.   You think so?

OTHER WOMAN.   Think so?—Yes.

How broad his chest is!—Look!—and how it
heaves!
Hard work, I think, but thrilling work as
well,
To keep inside of it a spirit grand
As his!

BACCHINA.   Note you his graceful limbs, and
how

He poises at the waist, as if about
To leap to some fair realm of beauty which
His flesh enrobes but cannot realize!

CAVALCANTI (*to* DANTE *at the extreme Left Front*).

One whose position lifts him where the crowd

Look up to him should never use the station
To drag up low down brutes like this Donati.

DANTE. I only spoke the truth.

CAVALCANTI. Cook soup for swine!
They leave you, if they fail to find it swill;
Or else, in greed to get it, trip and tramp you.
They harm you for your help; and still stay
swine.

DANTE. But surely I meant right.

CAVALCANTI. Perhaps you did;
But when we find men claiming they meant
right,
We find most others claiming they went
wrong.

DANTE. You doubt me?

CAVALCANTI. It were hard not doubting one
Who turns against his own.

DANTE. You mean?

CAVALCANTI. I mean
Exactly what I say. A little black,
If mixed with white, may soil the white as
much
As all black would.

DANTE. Yourself had been all black,
And lost for Florence all its liberty,
Had I myself not urged you to the fight.
'T is only justice, gratitude, to own it.

CAVALCANTI.　Unjust, ungrateful, am I?—What
　　are you

　　To fling these taunts at one who merely
　　　seeks

　　To snatch you from the toils of your own
　　　folly?

　　The world you think in is a world of fancy.

　　The world all live in is a world of fact.

　　　　　*Exit—Left Front—*CAVALCANTI.

(DANTE *looks after him, then takes out his manu-*
　　　　script and writes.

DONATI (*to* SIMONE, *and looking toward* DANTE
　　and CAVALCANTI).

　　They must have quarreled.

SIMONE.　　　　　　　　　Yes, it looks like that.

DONATI.　It does; and, when our enemies fall
　　out,

　　'T is time that we ourselves fall in.　For then

　　They fight for their own cause with half their
　　　force,

　　And with the other half they fight for us.

SIMONE.　I judge 't was Cavalcanti's jealousy

　　That caused the jar.

DONATI.　　　　　　　And their twin poet-natures.

　　When minds are filled so full of light conceits,

　　Clipped off like chippings from substantial
　　　concepts,

They store fit kindling-wood, when comes a
    friction,
To burst in flame. You know I always hold
A dreaming man is not a dangerous foe;
For dreams portend their opposites. Just
    when
He wings his whims to heaven, he wakes in
    hell.
Ay, ay, a foe deficient in his brain
Is quicker vanquished than if so in body;
For he whose reason fails him in the fray
Fights like a knight unbuckling his own mail.
    *Exeunt—Right Front—*DONATI *and* SIMONE.
(GEMMA *and* BACCHINA *who have been near the
    Right Upper approach* DANTE.)
BACCHINA (*to* DANTE). You know how all are
    talking of you? Oh,
Your ears must flame!
DANTE (*putting his manuscript in his pocket*).
               If flaming high enough,
I might then look like Moses.
BACCHINA.   But suppose
 They talked against you?
DANTE.   I would act like him.
BACCHINA. Be meek?
DANTE.   Oh, yes; as meek as he was when
He took down Aaron's calf.

BACCHINA. Whose calf is here?

DANTE. Why theirs who rather would look back to Egypt

Than forward to a promised land.

GEMMA. You mean
The poet's land?

DANTE. It might mean that to you.

BACCHINA. Why not?—The poet's is the promised land,—

Is always promised, but it never comes.

GEMMA. Some think that he would fly to it.

DANTE. Why not?
Some minds would walk and some would fly. You fear

That those who fly all fail to leave a footprint?

GEMMA. You seem despondent. You have quarreled—eh?—

With Cavalcanti?

DANTE. We exchanged some words.

BACCHINA. And flung them hard to make them hurt the thing

They hit, not so?—They made your faces red.

DANTE. The day is warm—and pleasant.

BACCHINA *laughs and turns away.*

*Exit—Right Front—*BACCHINA *and* OTHER WOMAN.

GEMMA. Should be; yes—
  For one like you, whom it has proved a hero.
DANTE. A hero?
GEMMA. That is what the whole town says.
DANTE. I did but do my duty.
GEMMA. That is what
  But very few do. It gave you your chance.
DANTE. So pigmies, did one plod with them,
    might give
  A little common man a chance of greatness.
GEMMA. Of course.
DANTE. Well, I would rather work with
    giants.
GEMMA. Why?
DANTE. They could lift me up above myself.
GEMMA. But you—you do not need that.
DANTE. Not?—Not I?—
  When I am lingering here to learn from you?
GEMMA. My uncle and the people—you have
    heard them—
  Would all give you an uplift.
DANTE. When the heart
  Sinks deep as mine, touch deft enough to reach
    it
  Requires a single hand, not many.
GEMMA. You
  Intend to flatter?

DANTE. Do I?

GEMMA. You appear
To question me.

DANTE. One never questions—does he?—
A thing in which he takes no interest?

*Enter—Left Upper—*CAVALCANTI *and* BEATRICE,
and stand watching them.

GEMMA. I interest you then?

DANTE. Yes, all things do.

GEMMA. That holds no flattery.

DANTE. What?—to treat a maid
As if confounding her with all things?

GEMMA (*looking toward the Right Front*). There
My uncle comes. I think would speak to you.
*Exeunt—Right Front—*DANTE *and* GEMMA.

BEATRICE (*looking after them*). He seems atten-
tive to her.

CAVALCANTI. Yes, and goes
To meet Donati.

BEATRICE. Is it she, or he,
That draws him toward the Blacks?

CAVALCANTI. No fish are
drawn
Except by hooks first baited to their taste.

BEATRICE. He has a taste then for your enemies?

CAVALCANTI. I do not know.

BEATRICE. You doubt him?

CAVALCANTI. No; I mourn him.

BEATRICE. You may be right. 'T is hard to make him out.

CAVALCANTI. And harder, if you make him out, to say it.

At times, us men who think we understand him

He welcomes but like strangers pushing in

The front door of one's house before they knock.

BEATRICE. His poems plead with me, his lips with her.

His brain seems like a bat's at blazing noon

That works but to work out some inward whim

And aims at nothing. [18]

CAVALCANTI. Nay; it aims at all things.

Perhaps it might be wise to let him know

Your judgment of him.

BEATRICE. How could that be done?

CAVALCANTI. If when one come to pluck a rose, he finds

It grows on thorns, he may become more cautious.

BEATRICE. Would that be friendly?

CAVALCANTI. Are our foremost friends

The ones who first forget our faults, or fail
Of effort to correct them?

BEATRICE.   Did we turn
Our preferences to pedagogues, and school
The souls that came to us for sympathy,
Though best of friends, we might seem worst
of foes.

*Enter—Right Front—*DANTE *followed by* CINO.

CAVALCANTI. We quarreled lately. Notice me
ignore him.

    (CAVALCANTI *and* BEATRICE *pass* DANTE
*without bowing to him although they bow
to* CINO. DANTE *sits in distress on the
bench* [19].)

*Exeunt—Right Front—*CAVALCANTI *and* BEA-
TRICE.

CINO (*to* DANTE, *sitting down beside him*).
What is it?

DANTE.   Why, you saw! They were
my friends.
Oh what a world is this for souls to live in!—
For spirits whose one deepest wish it is
To think at one with others like themselves,
And all together think one thought of God!
But here one knows no wishes not imprisoned
Where all the implements to set him free

Are but these clumsy tools of breath and
　brawn.

CINO.　Some understand us.

DANTE.　　　　　　You, perhaps, not me!—
　My soul is but an alien on the earth,
　And alien most to this brute frame of mine
　That never lets me do the thing I would;
　So what I like not, it attracts to me;
　And what I like and love, it drives away.

CINO.　This on the day the people cheered you so?

DANTE.　You think I craved their cheering?
　　No, not that.
　I only want the best I have within
　To be made better and believed, and then
　Received by those about me.

CINO.　　　　　　　　They all know
　How you have fought for Florence.

DANTE.　　　　　　　Do they know
　How I would have them live, so none should
　　need
　To fight for her? Think you 't is by the sword
　That one can set a soul, while living, free?
　Ah, not by deeds but dreaming does the spirit,
　Itself uplifted, lift up those about it.

CINO.　So you remain a poet!

DANTE.　　　　　　　I remain
　What heaven has made me.

4

CINO. Does it come from
heaven?

DANTE. It comes from all in life that is worth
living.

*Enter—Left Upper—*TWO MESSENGERS *from the*
BLACKS.

Enter—Right Upper—A MESSENGER *from the*
WHITES.

MESSENGER FROM BLACKS (*to* DANTE, *who
with* CINO *rises*). Donati and the leaders
of the Blacks

Will dine to-night at Carpi's. They await
you.

MESSENGER FROM WHITES (*to* DANTE). And
Cavalcanti and the Whites will dine

At Rondinelli's. They await you, too.

MESSENGER FROM BLACKS. Our invitation was
the first.

MESSENGER FROM WHITES. And mine
The best.

MESSENGER FROM BLACKS (*drawing sword*).
Then prove it.

(*The other* MESSENGER FROM BLACKS *also draws
his sword.*)

MESSENGER FROM WHITES (*drawing sword*).
You are two to one;

And that is one too many.

DANTE (*drawing his sword to separate them*).
>   Here, fight fair!
MESSENGER FROM BLACKS.   You think your
>   own fair play—against my side
And back?
DANTE.   I would not harm you.   I would
>   keep
You both from harming one another.
MESSENGER FROM BLACKS.   Oh!
*Enter—Right Upper—*CAVALCANTI *and* BEA-
>   TRICE.
>   (DANTE *does not notice them*).
DANTE (*to* MESSENGERS).   No flattery for your-
>   selves!   In times like these
A man would kick apart the meanest curs
That snarled and snapped each other for the
>   bone
Beside the city gate, and so save all
That all might still keep watch for Florence.
MESSENGER FROM BLACKS.   Ah,
You think when you have cursed us all as curs
That this will keep the city's peace?
MESSENGER FROM WHITES.   Well, well;
No man that calls me cur but I call down.
CAVALCANTI.   What is it?   Wait here.
(*Motions to* MESSENGER OF WHITES *who falls
>   back*.)

BEATRICE.   I have sometimes heard [20]
  That whom the gods destroy they first make
    mad.
  What pity it would be, did Florence fall,
  Because of one defender less to save her!
  When foes assail our hights they all should
    look
  To find us marshalled here in unity
  With all our differences hid as deep
  As are the lowest things the valley shadows.
MESSENGER FROM WHITES.   You may be right.
MESSENGER FROM BLACKS (*sheathing his
  sword, as do also the others*).
                  Some things that may go wrong
  Are righted by the touch of circumstance.
CAVALCANTI. All things are righted by the
  touch of reason.
  Without it men are but base tools of passion,
  And all their world here, the abode of
    brutes.
DANTE (*to* MESSENGERS).   Your pardon, gentle-
  men; but I must dine
  In my own home to-night. I thank you
    much.
*Exeunt—Right Front—*CAVALCANTI, BEATRICE,
    and MESSENGER FROM WHITES.
*Exit—Left Front—*MESSENGERS FROM BLACKS.

DANTE (*to* CINO, *taking out his manuscript and looking towards* BEATRICE).

Do your wrists, ankles, thighs, and arms, all ache?

CINO. All ache?

DANTE. Yes, ache.

CINO. How so?

DANTE. They ache, I say!
At times with too much joy, as if a-tremble
To fly above, yet bound by brawn below;
Or when you feel insulted, slighted, sad,
They do not ache then, either?

CINO. No, not mine.

DANTE. You never feel your soul here in your nerves?

CINO. No, no.

DANTE. My nerves are weaker, then, than yours.

CINO. Your soul may then be stronger.

DANTE. Say not that.

CINO. And better!

DANTE. Nay; no friendship that is true
Was ever caught or kept by flattery.
No; I am weaker, maybe worse.

CINO. Take care!
The modest may be more unjust to self
Than are the egotistic to their fellows.

DANTE. If just or not just to myself, who knows
   it?
   Why even you, you do not feel as I do.
   Why should a soul, whose one wish is to be
   Akin with others—understood,—be made
   So different?
CINO (*pointing to* DANTE'S *manuscript*). My
      Dante, all the thoughts
   That flood the world spring up from single
      souls;
   And some of these may bless it most when
      made
   To spend their lives interpreting themselves.
   DANTE (*putting his manuscript in his pocket*).
   I thank you; but I fear that any soul
   That needs to be interpreted, before
   It gains the common love of common men—
   For this alone is all for which I long—
   Dwells in the doom of some uncommon
      curse.
CINO. Do not think that.
DANTE.   And wherefore should I not?
   Here stood two parties. Each I strove to
      serve.
   With what result?—a brawl befitting wolves,
   Till I, dishonored bone of their contention,
   Am snarled aside.

CINO.　　　　　An hour ago, they praised you.

DANTE.　What care I for the masses' praise or
　　blame?
　But larger atoms of earth's common dust,
　If whirled against one or away from one,
　They cannot fill or empty thus the sphere
　Where dwells the spirit.　Let them come or go.
　My soul desires not many things but much—
　Ah yes, and too much, too much, as it seems!

*Enter—Left Front—*GEMMA *and* OTHER WOMEN.

CINO (*looking toward them*).
　Is that what you desire?

DANTE.　　　　　　　You said just now
　The world could not interpret my desire.
　There is but one—and all things work to make
　My presence to that one misrepresent me.

GEMMA (*approaching with a garland in her hand,
　　and addressing* DANTE).
　Yes, it is brought for you.

DANTE.　　　　　For me?

GEMMA.　　　　　　　For you.
　The knight whose hard strife keeps our soil
　　our own,
　As much as gardeners who keep it growing,
　Deserves the garland that is got from it.

*Enter—Right Upper—*BEATRICE *and* CAVAL-
　　CANTI, *unseen by* DANTE.

DANTE (*to* GEMMA *and the* WOMEN, *as he takes
   the garland*).
  I thank you. Fitting too, it is that these
  That represent the beautiful in nature
  Should represent it, too, in human form.
  What man could fail to do his best to gain
  The city's best in symbol and in substance!
(*Bowing to* GEMMA, *then looking up and seeing*
   BEATRICE, *he suddenly sits on the bench.*) [2 1]
CINO (*bending over him*).   What is it?
DANTE.   Nothing.
CINO (*to the* OTHERS).   Nothing, so he says.
  Perhaps the battle had exhausted him.

CURTAIN.

ACT THIRD.

SCENE: *A Room in the House of* DANTE. *Against the back wall, nearest the Right Entrance, is a table, on two sides of which are chairs. Other chairs and a sofa are in the Room. Entrances by doors at Right and Left. The windows are closed and the light not bright.*

The rising Curtain reveals DANTE *and* CINO *sitting at the table.* DANTE *is listlessly looking away from the manuscript in front of himself; and* CINO *is diligently examining another.*

CINO (*looking toward* DANTE).
    Why, Dante, you have lost your interest?—
DANTE. I have.
CINO.   Your verse there is not new, of course.
    I got it from you months ago[4]; but yet
    True poems hold the truth as gems the light,
    When rightly polished drawing to their depth
    All that is luminous in earth or heaven;
    And thence reflect it not alone but flash it;
    And not till all light go, can lose their brilliance.

DANTE. You give the reason—all my light is
    gone.
  You still write poetry?

CINO.   Why, yes, and so
  Still need your criticism; ay, just now
  Have found a new task baffling me.

DANTE.   In what?

CINO. A sister of a friend of mine has died,—
  A maiden of such beauty, grace, and love,
  It were impossible to think her dead,
  And not be drawn toward beauty, grace, and
    love
  In their diviner aspects.

DANTE.   You should write
  Of her?

CINO. So have I thought; but what or how?—
  Perhaps you might suggest it. [22]

DANTE.   Cino, Cino,
  I understand you.   There are souls on earth
  With senses all so fine and penetrant
  That no thoughts in a kindred soul can lie
  So deeply hidden that they stand not naked.
  Not her you mean; not you it is need help.
  You mean my own lost love.   You mean my-
    self.
  You think that hearts too heavy weighed with
    grief

May empty through their words as well as
   tears.
I thank you, Cino. Let my tears flow
   first.
Our sorrows are half lifted when the souls
Of our true friends have come to bear them
   with us.
Last night when darkness fell and veiled my
   face [23]
From those I surely thought it else had
   frighted,
I walked the streets and watched the city
   dream.
In lanes, in inns, in churches, and in homes
Each face I gazed at loomed as grim with
   shadows
As those that clung to mine. Her funeral
   pall
Seemed closely hung about myself as her,
Flopping a dangling, dire, bedraggled fringe
Of tear-soaked black between myself and all
   things.
Cino. Think not she lies beneath it. Nay, she
   lives;
And lives where all may look for inspiration.
Dante. The one sure proof of inspiration is
   That it inspires. I feel no inspiration.

CINO.   The air of heaven to-day is full of sun-
  shine.
  Shut in here do you feel it?   No; none do
  But those who journey forth to do life's work.
  Their lot were yours, were you to follow them.
      Knocking at the Left Entrance.
      DANTE *and* CINO *both rise.*
      *Enter—Left—*ATTENDANT.
          He hands DANTE *a Card.*
DANTE.   Excuse me, Cino.   I must calm my-
  self—
  Will soon return.   A man should not look
  grieved
  To greet a friendly visitor.
      *Exit—Right—*DANTE.
The ATTENDANT *opens the door at the Left
      Entrance.*
      *Enter—Left—*CAVALCANTI.
CINO (*to* CAVALCANTI).   Good day.
      *Exit—Left—*ATTENDANT.
CAVALCANTI (*bowing to* CINO).   I have not seen
  him lately—never since
  The death of Beatrice—
CINO.   That seemed to quench
  All ardor in him for all work.
CAVALCANTI.   I hope.
  But temporarily.   A mind like his

Glows like a spark upon a wintry hearth,—
The brightest promise that the times afford.

CINO. Vitality as buoyant as his own
Can hardly sink. Yet, whelmed in floods of
  grief,
All men at times have need of helping hands.

CAVALCANTI. The hand that helps another most
  is his
Whose own hand would find help.

CINO. Let him know
The help that Florence needs.

CAVALCANTI. The loss he feels
Is like the love it followed, less derived
From outward traits discovered in another,
Than inward temperament revealed in self.
Can any outward substitute replace
That which was all within?—But we can try it.

CINO. He comes, I see.

*Enter—Right—*DANTE.
He exchanges bows with CAVALCANTI.

CAVALCANTI. So sorry for you, friend.

DANTE. I find me in life's path, a traveler
Whom accident has maimed, and would be left
To die, did friends not come to rescue him.

CAVALCANTI. Ay, but they do come!

DANTE. Yes, I thank you, yes;
And yet, what can they do for one?

CINO. Perhaps
Their outstretched hands may show that love
is hidden
Behind the mysteries that seem to cloak it.

DANTE. I thank you, Cino.

CINO. Dante, I believe,
Though hard the drill that trains the soul to
read it,
That every message of the stars is written
In letters one can learn to spell on earth.

DANTE. Oh, I can do but little now with letters!

CAVALCANTI. It seems thus to you.

DANTE. Seems thus, Cavalcanti?—
And what is life except the thing that seems?
There was a time this round horizon rested
About my spirit, as about my finger
This ring of gold; and in it gleamed a gem
That centered all heaven's light, and flashed it
forth.
That gem is lost. With it my light is lost.

CAVALCANTI. I hope not, Dante. Florence yet
is left.

DANTE. Alas for Florence!

CAVALCANTI. There are those who
claim
Her destined to receive the help of Rome?

DANTE. How so?

CAVALCANTI. What we are asking. No one
    knows.

CINO. A mystery yet! The Church has not
    revealed it.

CAVALCANTI. Too much a mystery! When men
    distrust
  Their own thought or their thought's authority
  So they disguise it all in robes of office,
  Which only men are bid to honor, then
  I fear they hide what no man ought to honor.

CINO. You are a skeptic, Cavalcanti.[9]

CAVALCANTI. Yes;
  As long as one thing in the world is wrong,
  Some skeptic should be here to think it so.

DANTE. Has no one tried to solve the mystery?

CAVALCANTI. To question mysteries guarded by
    the Church
  Does not provoke safe answers in our time.

DANTE. Can no one solve it but the Church?

CAVALCANTI.   I fear
  Donati could; and therefore say I fear.

      *Enter—Left—*ATTENDANT *with a card.*

DANTE (*taking the card and reading it*). Why,
    even now, Donati visits me.
  Will you excuse me?

CAVALCANTI.   Ay, but may the comer
  Be levied to bear tribute to our quest.

DANTE. Will see you later.

CAVALCANTI. Yes, farewell.

CINO. Farewell.

*Exeunt—Right—*CAVALCANTI *and* CINO.

The ATTENDANT *opens the door at the Left.*

*Enter—Left—*DONATI, SIMONE, *a* PRIEST,
GEMMA, *and an Elderly* CHAPERON.

*Exit—Left—*ATTENDANT.

DONATI (*to* DANTE). When passing, though by
accident,

The loyal pause to honor royalty,

So we to honor one whom we esteem.

DANTE. I thank you. You are welcome.

(*All exchange greetings.*)

Will you sit?

(*They bow, but they do not sit.*)

DONATI (*to* DANTE). We have not met you
lately.

DANTE. No.

PRIEST. You think,

You poets, you are called to testify

To what incites you from within, and so

The less you take from outside life the better?

DANTE. At times, if aimed for better poetry.

PRIEST. Oh, say not that!

DANTE. Why not?

PRIEST. If it would grow,

A nature young as yours has need of health.
The spirit's health is hope.   Without it none
Attain full manhood.   Life is like a day.
It wakes to longer work and larger wage,
The brighter its beginning.

DANTE.   Yes, I fear so.

PRIEST.   You fear so, eh?—and yet you do not fear
  Insulting nature when it comes to bless you
        (*Pointing to the closed shutters*)
  With windows barred like this, as if the day
  Had brought not light but lances.

DANTE.   Think I need it?

DONATI.   At least, enough light from the outer world
  To see what now has come to Florence.

DANTE.   What?

DONATI.   The Holy Father's promise and protection
  Against the Emperor.

DANTE.   Is it true?

DONATI.   It is.

PRIEST.   And that would bring the whole our city needs,—
  Not strength so much to fight the force without
  But spirit to unite the force within.
  Life grows here like a tree with outer branches

s

Too broad for any handling, but with trunk
So small and slender that a single hand
Can fix its destiny for life or death.
The trunk of all that lives is in the spirit.
But find the hand that can be laid on
    that,
You find what brings to all things bloom or
    blight.

DANTE. You mean the Holy Father's?

PRIEST.   I mean his.
With outer facts we merely fashion faction,
In inner feeling we find fellowship.

DONATI. He speaks the truth.

DANTE.   Ay, what a noon were that!
There were no shade beside a thing on
    earth,
If heaven's one sun were central over all.
You think it could be done?—could end our
    factions?

DONATI. Why could it not?—not many men
    would band
Against the Holy Father.

DANTE. And were you—
Were you the source whence came this con-
    summation?

DONATI. So men have said.

DANTE.   And will you pardon me?

In thought, if not in word, my lack of knowledge
Had lacked the honor due you.

DONATI. You are frank.

PRIEST. A mind with thought forever in the
clouds
May be excused for stumbling, now and then,
At what, if seen through, might appear mere
shadow.

GEMMA. One may excuse a bird, if, when it
flies,
It fails in seeing everything on earth. [24]

DANTE. I beg your pardon, lady—for I fear
To court with too much courtesy the truth
That but to be truth bids us oft be curt—
Some poet's eyes are keen as are their fellows!
In searching through the pathways of the past,
What guide men better in their task than
poems?

SIMONE. But how about the future?

DANTE. 'T is in them
One reads the most of that which is to come.

SIMONE. And in the present, too?

DANTE. In it, not that
Which is but should be, is the poet's theme,
And he who thinks it thinks the thought of
God.

DONATI. Come, come, we need not quarrel.
 Not how men
  Can fight the air with words, but how their
   frames
  Can back their words with blows that free
   their air
  Of all that blocks right doing, this is that
  By which a man reveals his worth in life.
  And you will join with us, and with the
   Church?

DANTE. You may depend upon me.

DONATI.   That I shall
   (*aside to* SIMONE).
  Now we shall have but half the Whites against
   us.
   (*to* DANTE).   I must be going to my offices.
   (*to* GEMMA).   You said, I think, that you
  go elsewhere?

GEMMA.   Yes.

DONATI (*to* DANTE).   'T is time we leave you.

DANTE (*bidding good-bye to* DONATI, SIMONE,
    and OTHERS).
  Thank you for your visit.

Exeunt—Left—DONATI, SIMONE, PRIEST, *and*
              ATTENDANTS.

   (*to* GEMMA).
  They seemed in haste.

GEMMA. Are bent on business.

DANTE. You know, I sometimes think that business
  Is like a cyclone, fills our ways with dust
  And bustle; yet men say it comes to clear them
  And bring us rest and comfort. Humph!—farewell.

GEMMA. So kind in you to help my uncle!²⁴

DANTE. No;
  My heart belongs to Florence; only beats
  That she may live her life; and he was kind
  In helping her; and I have gratitude.
  Ay, he was right. For us one hope remains,—
  The Church. We both look forward to the Church,
  And, joined by it, our union will be perfect.

*Enter—Right—*CAVALCANTI *and* ATTENDANTS.
      They overhear the last sentence.

Exeunt—Left—after exchanging farewells, GEMMA
            and CHAPERON.

DANTE (*turning to* CAVALCANTI).
  Ah, back again?

CAVALCANTI. We are.

DANTE. Have news?

CAVALCANTI. We had.

DANTE. What was it?

CAVALCANTI. Nay, like wise men, we are wary
  Of friends that follow those with hostile colors.
DANTE. I do not see—
CAVALCANTI. We saw and heard and know.
DANTE. Oh that was nothing!
CAVALCANTI. Not for you, perhaps.
  But very much for us.
DANTE. Let me explain.
CAVALCANTI. You need not; nor excuse it. Temperament
  And taste, like flower and fragrance, go together.
  What God hath joined let man not put asunder.
DANTE. But you——
CAVALCANTI. Have found before that family reasons,
  At times, turn white to black.
DANTE. Are no such reasons.
CAVALCANTI. Mere words are wind; nor all their storm or stress
  Can pack the air so thought cannot see through it.
DANTE. You mean?

CAVALCANTI.   We overheard

DANTE.   And think—

CAVALCANTI.   And know.

DANTE.   To know one needs to learn.   How did
    you learn?—

  What steps were those that led up to your
    knowledge?

CAVALCANTI.   When mortals climb a path to
    truth unseen,

  They feel their way along the links of logic.

DANTE.   Aha!

CAVALCANTI.   The notes just heard from you
    but echo

  The strains that all have heard you pipe for
    months.

DANTE.   Why then have I myself not heard the
    echoes?

CAVALCANTI.   I take you, Dante, for a man of
    honor. [18]

  And after prying, pulling, plucking, plying,

  With such a maiden's heart, you would not
    fling

  The soiled thing back to her, face us, and
    claim

  You had been empty handed? [18]

DANTE.   Cavalcanti!

  And you, of all men, knew the thing I meant.

CAVALCANTI. The thing you said!—To God
    with what you meant!—
  One who has not His confidence must guess it.
DANTE. How did my spirit trip to fall so low
    In your esteem?
CAVALCANTI.   We mortals are compounded
    Of sense below, and spirit resting on it.
  If sense give way, no wonder spirit falls.
DANTE. You deem me treacherous to the one
    above
  That so I love; and treacherous too to one 25
  That I do not love?—By your hope of heaven,
  In your deep heart, can you believe this of
    me?
CAVALCANTI. Why, think you, some men call
    me skeptical?—
  Because I say what I believe, not so?
DANTE. But do you think?—
CAVALCANTI.   What else, pray, could
    one think?—
  You just took council with Donati.
DANTE.   There!—
  Again your jealousy! He called on me,
  Not I on him.
CAVALCANTI. You knew his object?
DANTE.   Yes—
  To end our factions for us here in Florence,—

To place above us all the sovereignty
Which only brings good will and peace on
    earth.
CAVALCANTI. And you have pledged yourself
    and followers
To join Donati in enthroning this?
DANTE. I have.
CAVALCANTI. You fool.
DANTE.   Take care.
CAVALCANTI.   I say but truth.
A man who fails to judge the character
Of what is promised by the character
Of him who promises, reveals no mind;
For mind is what connects effect and cause.
You knew the baseness of Donati, yet
Guessed not the baseness that was in his plan.
Henceforward, though you know a bush be
    poison,
Bid men come pluck and gorge its pretty ber-
    ries;
And, if all die, expect no blame for it—
You have but carried out the kind of thought
With which heaven filled the kind of mind like
    yours.
Surrender, would you, to the Holy Father?[26]
You know what that means?—All his troops
    come armed.

Their leader is the French prince, Charles
  of Valois.

The Emperor, I tell you, is a very god

Beside a devil of a man like Charles,—

A treacherous, truthless, crafty, cruel brute;

Who too comes pledged to slaughter or to
  banish

Each man of us not in Donati's faction.

DANTE. Can this be true?

CAVALCANTI. It is. May heaven defend us!

The pull that lifts one by a rotting rope

Is far less dangerous than the help that comes

From foolish friends.

*Enter, suddenly—Left—*DONATI, SIMONE, PRIEST,
                and ATTENDANTS.

DONATI (*noticing* CAVALCANTI *and* ATTEND-
    ANTS).

       Aha! They would dissuade you?

DANTE. There seems a difference of opinion
    here.

DONATI. I have your promise.

CAVALCANTI.   And I fear a traitor.

DONATI (*to* DANTE). And he has given you
    proof?

CAVALCANTI (*to* DONATI). What need of proof?

We best can judge of some things by their
    source,—

Of days by daylight, and of good by goodness.
Heaven sends the one, and only heavenly
    traits
Can bring the other.

DONATI (*to* CAVALCANTI).   Yours are heavenly
    traits?—
He made a promise.   Now you bid him break
    it?

CAVALCANTI.   A promise made to suit a lie but
    robes
Untruth that truth should strip and so show
    naked.

DONATI.   Here stand my men; and if his tongue
    prove false,
           (*pointing toward* DANTE)
Their blades know how to cut it loose from
    him.

CAVALCANTI.   And here stand mine; and if he
    prove a traitor,
Their blades know how to cut him loose from
    us.

DONATI (*to* DANTE).   Now choose between us,
    if you dare.

CAVALCANTI.   Ay, choose!

DANTE.   Have you considered that to which
    you dare me?
To start right here a civil war in Florence?

Kill off our bravest citizens, and open
The doors of half our homes to lust and mur-
   der?
And do you think that I could dare do that?
You bid me choose between you.   You forget
There is another power upon the earth
Far higher, stronger, than can be your own.
      (*placing his hand on the* PRIEST)
I hide beneath the shelter of the church.
I vow a pilgrimage to Rome; and thus
        (*turning to* DONATI)
Fulfil my promise,
         (*turning to* CAVALCANTI)
              and find out the truth
From him who knows it best,—the Holy
   Father.[27]

       CURTAIN.

ACT FOURTH.

SCENE: *A Monk's Cell. It is dimly lighted by a single lamp, and is connected by a door with a church, from which the sound of musical instruments and of singing can be heard. The cell is plainly furnished with three or four chairs or benches. In the Right Rear is an alcove in front of which hangs a Curtain. This can be opened fully, or only partly, revealing then a space, through which, at times, indicated in the text, a moving head and bust can be seen.*

Entrances, Right and Left, the latter into the church.

*Enter—Left—*DANTE *and* CINO, *shutting the door and making the cell darker.*

DANTE. My journey wrought no good. The
    Holy Father

    Kept me a prisoner there for months, you
      know,[27]

    For fear my presence here should thwart his
      purpose;—

    Was courteous, of course; but Cavalcanti

    Was more than half-way warranted, I fear.

In Church or State, the official seems the
    same,—
A fist in front with which to threaten one;
A palm behind to beg him for a bribe.

CINO.   Yet you yourself are prior of the city?

DANTE.   And so have learned that when men
    give us votes,
They lie in wait to have their gifts returned,—
To wrest from us an undeserved reward,
Or brand us ingrates whom all friends desert.

CINO.   Oh, say not all!

DANTE.   No, Cino, no; not all. [28]
Forgive me, Cino.   Since we two were boys,
The only love that I have felt returned,
Has been my love for you.

CINO.   And yet they say
The love of woman——

DANTE.   Could that satisfy
And thrill with aught so true, unselfish,
    pure?—
I worship boyhood, thinking what we were.

CINO.   But what of Rome?

DANTE.   If leading toward the wrong,
Ought those who seek the right to follow her?

CINO.   Good children follow.

DANTE.   Parents gone insane,
Or but awry, are saved by opposition.

Love uniformed and forced in hatred's press-
    gang
Is only served by those who war against it.
Our thoughts of good should learn to separate
The heavenly love from its foul earthly nest.
To hold the latter's dead impurity
At one with spotless life that wings on high,
Is often to deserve—I will not judge them.
I would I could forget them. Do you know
Some men there are have murder in their
    hearts
Through all their lives; and if they murder
    not——

CINO. They may be rightly numbered with the
    saints.
Not what our lower nature makes us feel,
But what our higher nature lets us do,
Determines what we are.

DANTE.   I hope so, friend.
At times my soul appears a stormy sea,
All rage below and rain above; and then
It seems the tears I shed have drained me dry,
And left a void too deep for faith in God
Or man to fill.

CINO   For that I brought you here.

DANTE. And kindly meant, but yet we mortals
    find

That few things, when we turn them inside
   out,
Are proved to be the miracles we thought
   them.

CINO. But you may see here for yourself.

DANTE.   Oh no!
The time to see the feathers on a wing
Is not the while it flies; no, no; and not
While playing sleight of hand to see the
   fingers.

CINO. But you can use your judgment.

DANTE.   No, again!—
No man who is no expert risks a judgment
On questions experts only can decide,
Without revealing his own lack of judgment.

CINO. At least, your mind is open.

DANTE.   Yet to what?—
All brains with limits are what polyps own
You think?—Ours too fit forms whose grasp
   can never
Outreach the touch of short tentacula.
Your monk has credit here?[29]

CINO.   With some he has.
They think that through him they have seen
   the Virgin.

DANTE. Humph! He is coming.

*Enter—Right—*MONK.

CINO (*to* MONK).

I have brought with me
This gentleman—is prior of the city.

MONK. You do me honor.

CINO. Would consult with you
About the city's welfare.

MONK. I know not
What may be granted. Sometimes at this
hour,
The while one hears the music in the church,
I sink unconscious. Then, so am I told,
Some higher power proclaims its presence
through me.

*Music is heard from the church with the following
words:*

The sky contains full half I see.
In soil below I live, I love.
High in the half that looms above,
Oh, is there nothing there for me?

During the music, the MONK *points to the
curtain.* CINO *and* DANTE *draw it aside,
and examine the walls and floors behind
and beneath; then the* MONK *goes into
the alcove and draws the curtain behind
him. The words of the song are followed
by a soft instrumental interlude.*

6

DANTE. Seems honest.

CINO.   I have thought so.

DANTE.   Could one solve
All motives and all means of mystery,
There were no sphere for faith.

CINO.   No.   Sit you here.

> CINO *and* DANTE *take seats at the Left, facing the Curtain. Throughout the séance,* DANTE, *now and then, writes in his manuscript.*

DANTE. And now you think the prior of the city
May meet an actual Holy Father, eh?

After the instrumental interlude the following is sung:

> The sky's bright sun and stars I see
>   The soil below is guised in green
>   In heaven whose orbs are robed in sheen,
> Oh, is there nothing there for me?

> *These words are followed by a soft instrumental interlude. The curtain begins to move from side to side. Then it opens and a woman's form enrobed in a white gown appears.*

CINO. That seems a woman.

DANTE.   But the monk was beardless.

CINO. Yet note how slim she is.

DANTE. She may be, yes.

FIGURE. Good evening, friends.

DANTE. A very good falsetto!

The figure after making gestures disappears.

CINO. Well done, not so?

DANTE. Too well!

CINO. Could you explain it?

DANTE. Why no; not wholly. What of that? At times,

That facts are facts is plain without explaining.

To know things grow, we need not know their methods.

To think things handiwork, we need not see

The hand that does the work. What was she, think you?—

And what her object?

CINO. Was a guide preparing The way for more.

DANTE. Conducting spirit, eh?

After the instrumental interlude the following is sung:

In thoughts within, sweet rest I see;
　In things without, but dust and toil.
　Where hang no veils of flesh and soil,
Oh, is there nothing there for me?

> *These words are followed by a soft instrument-*
> *al interlude. The curtain opens, and*
> *a man's figure clothed in white appears.*

CINO. Watch that now.

DANTE.   Has a beard, and well
put on.

FIGURE. The world keeps rolling on from day to
night.

None always dwell where always glows the
light.

When darkness comes, and doubt assails the
mind,

Then light and faith come following swift behind.

> *The figure disappears.*

DANTE. Is optimistic. Yet the merest child
Could recognize the monk there by his
voice.

And what was he?

CINO.   A guide.

DANTE.   Another, eh?—
And learned his lesson well. But when will
those

That need the guiding come?

CINO.   Must wait and watch.

> *After the instrumental interlude the following is*
> *sung:*

In faith and hope and love I see
   Why earth sent home the Christ that came.
   When I go home, and own the same,
Shall there be nothing there for me?

These words are followed by a soft instru-
    mental interlude. The curtain opens and
    a figure of Beatrice clothed in white ap-
    pears.

CINO. Look there. I think your name was
   called too.

DANTE.   Yes,—
   And shall I answer?

CINO.   I would—go and see it.

DANTE (*rising and approaching the curtain*).

   Why, why,—what is it?—Cino, can you help
   me?

   Come here, please, come.

CINO.   Why, that is Beatrice.[30]

DANTE. You see her?

CINO.   Yes.

DANTE.   And it is not my fancy?

CINO. Nay, question not yourself, but her—
   less loud!—

   She else may disappear.

DANTE (*to the* FIGURE). You come to me?

FIGURE. And do you know me then?

DANTE.   Are Beatrice?—

You wear her form.—What would you have me
do?—

FIGURE. Do what you dreamt last night, and
now design.

DANTE. And then, what then?

FIGURE (*disappearing*). Then—we shall meet
again.

DANTE. Wait, wait! (*to* CINO) Why, call her
back!

CINO.   No, not to-day.

You spoke too loud.   Hear that?—The monk
is waking.

DANTE. Why I—I had no chance to test its
truth.

CINO. And yet you saw her.

DANTE.   Yes.

CINO.   And so did I.

DANTE. And if I come again here, can I see
her?

Enter—from behind the curtain—the MONK.

DANTE *continues, addressing the* MONK,

What I have seen now, can I see again?

MONK. They tell me so.   And did you get the
thought

To guide you in the conduct of the city?

DANTE. The conduct of?—Oh yes, you thought
of that?

(*to* CINO).

But as I sat here, I had not that thought,
But one sweet thought of her, and how to
　reach her;
And what it was that filled the space between
　us;
And how I could describe it! Did you hear
The word she spake. She bade me tell my
　dream
Of moving toward and meeting her.—But how
Could she have known it! Could I but be-
　lieve
She was a spirit sent here to inspire me!

　　(*to* MONK).

And you will let me come again, and prove
The truth of this?

MONK. 　　　　　I will; yet now it seems
That you believe it.

DANTE. 　　　　　With my heart I do.

MONK. And sometimes hearts judge better than
　do heads.

CINO. Ay, sometimes things may be so beauti-
　ful,
And fill the spirit with such holy thrills,
To doubt them were akin to doubting God,
When face to face with his own blazing pres-
　ence.

MONK. At least, all beauty changes what it
    brightens.

 A flower that blooms may merely fall to soil,
 But, when it does, the soil to which it falls
 Is never quite the same it was before.

DANTE. Yet mind has methods that must be
    fulfilled.

 You say that I may come again. I thank you.
    (*to* CINO).

 To save mine honor that men else had
    doubted, [18] [25] [31]

 I had to marry; yet I feared I wronged
 The memory of this other. Now, if true—
 Oh Cino, think!—She may forgive and guide
    me!

    *Enter—Left—*ATTENDANT *and* GEMMA.

They open the door and leave it open, letting in
much more light.

 Sh—sh—my wife.

(*gesturing and speaking to both* CINO *and the*
MONK).

            No word of this to her!

GEMMA (*bowing to others and speaking to* DANTE).

 I came here to attend the funeral—[32]
 Signora Frescobaldi. Then I learned
 That you had crossed the cloister. You should
    know

The threatened danger.   Whites and Blacks
  have come

In crowds and companies, all frowns and
  threats.

DANTE.   They surely have not brought their
  weapons?

GEMMA.   Yes.

DANTE.   Good God!—to treat His house as if
  a hot-house

To nursery blood-red blades of hellish hate!

We should prevent this.

MONK.   I will keep them parted.

          (*Holding up his cross.*)

Against the cross they will not dare to
  fight.

          *Exit—Left—*MONK.

DANTE.   The city-guards should be informed at
  once.

Here, take you this for me.

(*Writing on a manuscript and handing it to*
              ATTENDANT.)

          *Exit—Right—*ATTENDANT.

          (*A noise of conflict*).

CINO.   Already fighting?

     He moves toward the door at the Left.

Enter—Left—The MONK, *evidently slain, borne
          by* ATTENDANTS.

DANTE (*to* CINO, *as he himself kneels down to examine the* MONK *on the floor*).

Killed him? killed him?—and I can learn no more?—

The gates of heaven that he could set ajar,
And he alone, must now be closed again?

    *Enter—Left—*CAVALCANTI *and* DONATI, *both respectively followed by* WHITES *and* BLACKS. DANTE *rises and continues to them.*

Oh you accursed heathen! worse than those
Who ignorantly crucified the Lord!

You knew his messenger, yet murdered him.

ATTENDANT OF CAVALCANTI. It was an accident.

DANTE.   An accident!—

Like that which follows from the rock that falls

Where men who lie in wait have loosened it.

An accident—oh yes!—that plots to arm
The palsied, shaking, thought-void clutch of rage,

And let it loose to raise a hellish storm
Just where the good have come for heavenly calm!

The lightning of your flashing blades fell not
By accident.

ATTENDANT OF CAVALCANTI.   It was Donati's
 men
 That started it.
ATTENDANT OF DONATI.   Nay, Cavalcanti's.
DANTE.   Nay,
 But both; and all whose orders brought these
  arms.
 When mortals are our hosts, the meanest
  men
 Will not insult them in their homes, but you
 Come here to God's house, all equipped to break
 His law of love, and kill his ministers.
 Why, one might almost visit hell to-day
 In safety,—so deserted by the fiends
 Called out to take possession here of you!
 (*Some draw swords and some threaten him.*)
 You threaten me?—Why not?—Just now in
  there
    (*pointing toward the Left*)
 Were threatening God!—And do I fear you?
  —No;
 I have no need.   The men who dare do right
 Enlist with God, who guards—or guides them
  home.
   Enter—Right—A file of city guards.
 There is one certain way to end these troubles.
 I had my doubt before.   The priors lack

One vote by which to banish both your lead-
    ers,—
Yes, Cavalcanti and Donati, both.[32]
GEMMA.   Nay, say not that!
DANTE.   I say that I shall give it;
    And clear my conscience, while I clear this air,
    And clean these foul and corpse-clogged lanes
       of Florence.
    Let this be done, her son's aspiring hope
    May picture outlines of her destiny
    In hues more bright and sweet than could be
       dreamed
    By any soul besmirched here and bestenched
    In blotches of your cursed Black and White.

CURTAIN.

ACT FIFTH.

SCENE: *The same as in Act Third. Backing, at the center, is a desk connected with a writing table. In the desk are many manuscripts in confusion; and near it, on the floor, a waste basket. In the room are chairs and sofas. The rising curtain reveals* DANTE *with pen in hand sitting before a manuscript on the desk, humming and drumming with his fingers, as if marking off time to some rhythm.*
Entrances—Right and Left.

*Enter—Right—*GEMMA.

GEMMA (*to* DANTE).   What are you doing?

DANTE.   Writing.

GEMMA.   Always writing.

DANTE. That is my mission.

GEMMA.   Not your business.

DANTE.   They differ?

GEMMA.   Yes.   One's mission, as a rule,
Is wrought alone; one's business with others.
Things done alone may but be done for self.
Things done with others may be done, too, for
them.

DANTE. True missions only serve the higher
    self.

GEMMA. Some people always think their own
    selves higher

Than are the selves of those about them.

DANTE.   Oh!—

You knew me as a poet when we married.

GEMMA. I knew you as a boy, too; and I
    thought

That when you grew you would become a
    man.

There was a time my uncle thought so, too.

He pictured you a hero and a leader.

Now none dare claim you as a follower.

DANTE. None dare?

GEMMA.   Who dares to have a follower

That stabs him in the back, as you have
    stabbed

Donati and your great friend, Cavalcanti?

DANTE. You know I try to follow what is right.

GEMMA. And never find the right save in your-
    self;

And, if you did, your endless cant and chatter

Knagged out like warnings from a rattler's
    tail

Would worry off your faction's foes before

You harmed them.

DANTE. So you think me wrong?

GEMMA. As all do.
Who vote you prior now? They tax your all
Like some plebeian. When you wish to work,
None care to wager wages on your doing.

DANTE. And my own household also turn
against me?

GEMMA. Besides descending to your disesteem,
Your wife should hanker, eh, and hunger too
To starve with you! [33]

(*Snatches and tears up the manuscript he is
writing.*)

DANTE (*trying, at first, to save his manuscript*).
And why do you do that?

GEMMA. To wake you up.

DANTE. One who writes out his dream
Must be awake already.

GEMMA. I would make
You realize it, so I tear it up.

DANTE. One dream was torn up long ago, I fear.
Why, Gemma, when I married you I judged
Your spirit by the beauty of its body;
And that seemed so at one with what I fan-
cied
I could not doubt that it would prove at one—
Could we but know each other, through and
through—

With all my soul that had conceived the
fancy.

GEMMA. 'T was not the first time life has proved
that poets

Are fools who judge their fancies to be facts.

DANTE. At times, my faith still thinks they
may be facts.

Our fancies are the children of the soul,

With rights of heritage as true as those

Of any other form of thought. If so,

Then their relationship may be as true—

Though how we never now can understand—

To that which mortals term reality.

GEMMA. Past hope! Still prating of the soul!—
as if

A man could take it out and measure it!

DANTE. The stature of the soul is measured by

The distance of its outgrowth over earth.

GEMMA. The outgrowth, eh?—explains your
misfit, does it?—

Oh yes!—you have outgrown your low surroundings?

DANTE. Why misinterpret me? I may not fit

The world I live in. Did the Christ fit his?

Could any man walk straight in paths of
earth,

Nor trespass on some crooked paths of others?

*Enter—Left—*ATTENDANT, *and behind him* DINO.

*Exit—Left—*ATTENDANT.

GEMMA *and* DANTE.　Good day.

DINO.　　　　　　　　Good day.

DANTE.　　　　　　　　　　　And is
there any news?

DINO.　There is, and bad.　I thought I ought to
warn you.

DANTE.　How so?

DINO.　　　　　　Donati is returning soon
With Charles of Valois, and the French to back
him.

DANTE.　The Whites will not be able to protect
us?

DINO.　The Whites have lost their leader.

DANTE.　　　　　　　　　　Cavalcanti
Can be recalled now, if Donati come.

DINO.　No, no; not he; he is beyond recall.

DANTE.　What mean you?

DINO.　　　　　　He was banished by the priors
To Sarzana.—It is the home of fevers.[3][2]
They welcomed him too warmly.　He is gone.

DANTE.　I never knew of fever raging there.

GEMMA.　As many go astray through ignorance
As through iniquity.　Ay, there are times
Wise rascals do less harm than righteous fools.

7

DANTE.   You speak like that to me, and now?
   Oh God!
  When all my soul sinks downward with the
   weight
  Of that dead body of my friend?—no pity?
  You know there was but one right thing to do.
  I could not let the good of this rash friend
  Outweigh the safety of the whole of Florence.
GEMMA.   And yet be sure the whole of Florence
   feels
  Less gratitude for you than grief for him.
  His friends, at least——
DANTE.   I see; and I who tried
  To meet out equal justice to a hoard
  In Church and State, all squirming here like
   worms
  To tomb their mates in dirt and mount upon
   them,
  Priests cursing people, people cheating priests,
  Whites boasting of white shrouds they trail
   behind them,
  Blacks of black funeral palls that follow them,
  And every one of them too mean to own
  One other man the equal of himself,—
  I stand the enemy of all.   Oh God!—
  Some spirits here may seek thy higher life,
  And help their fellows.   It is not for me.

Would I mount up, I find no wings for it,
I fall.

  *Enter—Left—*ATTENDANT *and* CINO.

   All exchange greetings.

   *Exit—Left—*ATTENDANT.

   (DANTE *continues to* CINO).

And you, too, come to bring bad tidings?

CINO. I bring this proclamation. It concerns
you.

   (*Handing a paper to* DANTE.)

DANTE (*taking the paper and looking at it*).

Who wrote it, and who sent it, and from
where?

CINO. It comes here from Donati and Prince
Charles.

They march against the city.

DANTE.   But the Whites.

CINO. We have no leader, and the most are flying.

DANTE. What says the proclamation?

CINO.   It names you,

And four besides you, summoned to appear [34]

And answer for extortion and rebellion

Against the Pope and Charles.

DANTE.   Extortion? What?—

For raising pence to keep the city's peace?—

Rebellion, towards the city's enemies?
Who charges that?

CINO.   It says here, "common fame."

DANTE.   What threatens those who fail to heed
   the summons?

CINO.   Their property shall all be confiscated,
   Themselves be banished, and, if caught in
      Florence,
   Be burned alive.

DANTE.   If I obey the summons
   And speak the truth, they will obtain their
      wish;
   I shall be caught in Florence.

CINO.   You should leave.

DANTE.   Too true! but, first—you are a lawyer,
   Dino—
   Draw up a paper, making over all
   My property to Gemma.

          (DINO *sits at the desk and writes.*)

CINO (*taking* DANTE *to extreme Left*).   Why
   not deed
   The property to some one else in trust?

DANTE.   Not safe!   If held as mine it might be
   doomed.
   Donati's niece could keep it for herself.

CINO.   She might not deed it back.

DANTE.   She would not take it

From her own children; and, you know, besides,
We men who wed incur a debt of honor.

CINO. But should that let one harm himself?

DANTE.   Why, honor
  Is in oneself, and so does not depend
  On anything another is or does.
        (*to* DINO).
  The paper will be ready soon, not so?
  I must prepare me, and will then return.
          *Exit—Right—*DANTE.

GEMMA (*to* DINO). You must be sure to make
  all clear and certain.

CINO (*to* GEMMA). What will you do without
  him?

GEMMA.   Humph!—not penance!
  We do that only to the ones we worship.

CINO. So women do not worship those they
  marry.

GEMMA. Not after they have married them.

CINO.   Why not?

GEMMA. They get too near them.

CINO.   Humph! but that depends
  On what one means. They can not get too
  near
  To any one in spirit.

GEMMA.   What is that?

Cino. That in us which has least of body in
　　it;
　And yet, like fire, may glow when bodies
　　meet,
　And make one's whole life luminous.

Gemma (*looking at him disparagingly*). A poet!

Cino. Yes; making poetry is practising
　The language of the spirit. I should like
　To learn to speak it altogether.

Gemma. 　　　　　　　　Should you?—
　That wish is what sends Dante now from Flor-
　　ence.

Cino. That wish is what sends Dante now from
　　Florence;
　I shall remember. May I quote you to
　　him?

Gemma. 'T will be so kind of you, reminding
　him of me!

　　　　　*Enter—Right—*Dante.

Dante (*to* Dino). The writing ready?

Dino (*rising and handing the paper to him*).
　　　　　　　　　　　　　Brief but clear.

Dante (*reading it*).
　I see—will sign it.
　　　(*to* Cino *and* Dino).
　　　　　　　　Will you witness for me?
　　　Dante, Cino, *and* Dino *sign*.

DANTE (*handing paper to* GEMMA).

There, Gemma, well nigh all I had is yours.

You show it to your uncle. He will guard you.

> (*Knocking outside.*)

CINO (*looking through the window backing at the Left*).

They seem Donati's men (*to* DANTE). They come to fetch you.

DANTE (*turning toward the door*). I——

CINO. No, you must not. (*Pointing to the Right*).

> Leave the other way,
And jump the garden fence there—in the rear.

DINO. And yet the streets are full of them.

CINO. Wait, wait!

> (*removing his own hood and cloak*).

All know your hood and cloak. Take mine. None think

Enough of these to stop and question them.

DANTE. First let me show myself; and make them sure

That I am here.

> (*thrusting his head from the window*).

> What is that you want?

VOICE. Yourself.

DANTE. The house is not in order. Wait.
The madam must get ready to receive you.
    (*to* CINO *and* DINO, *as he puts on* CINO's
    cloak and hood, after removing his own).
I thank you for your kindness, gentlemen.
    (*shaking hands with them*).
A last word to my children; then I go.

DINO. Where shall we find you.

DANTE. At Verona soon—
Will send a messenger.
    *Exit—Right—*DANTE *and* GEMMA.
       (*Knocking outside.*)

VOICE OUTSIDE. You keep us waiting.

CINO (*putting on* DANTE's *hood and cloak*).
They all will deem me Dante. Note how well
I imitate his voice.

DINO. Is danger!

CINO (*thrusting his head out of the window*).
                       Wait;
Wait till the madam—gets——

VOICE OUTSIDE. It was not her,
But you we want.

CINO. I know; but please be patient.
      (CINO *draws in his head.*)
      *Enter—Right—*GEMMA.

DINO (*to* GEMMA). Has left?

GEMMA. Will soon—

CINO (*looking about the room*).   How is it with
    his writing?

Should they discover aught—

GEMMA *moves towards* DANTE'S *desk,* CINO *fol-*
    lows and continues.

                    The speaking voice

Is like a church bell, mainly rung for service;

But writing made for sight is like a belfry,

And draws attention to one's need of service.

GEMMA (*pulling one from other disordered man-*
    uscripts, on the desk and tearing it, and then
    throwing the parts into a waste-basket).

Not much here,—only poems!

CINO.   Yes, but they—

GEMMA (*thrusting her hand apparently against*
    a pen that pricks it).

One could not get a pen—I mean a penny

For all of them.   I wish his notes could store

As much of point and sharpness, after—say—

His pen has left them, as they seem to, now.

(CINO *and* DINO *exchange looks as if not relish-*
    ing the remark.)

    Loud knocking at the door.

(GEMMA *indicates that there is nothing more in the*
    desk.)

CINO.   Now when they come, we all should bide
    by this,—

That it was I who wore this hood of Dante—
To keep the chill off; and (*to* GEMMA) are
   both your friends,
Who sped to tell you of Donati's coming.
We thus give Dante time.

DINO.   Has need of time,
Or else will quickly get eternity.
Shall let them in now, eh?
            (*moving toward the Left*).

CINO.   Ay, ay; but lend
Your eye to me, and arm too, if they press me.

DINO *opens the door at the Left, then apparently*
      opens another beyond it.

*Enter—Left—*SIMONE *and many* ATTENDANTS.
      They look around them, then besiege CINO,
         who is at the Right. CINO *draws his*
         sword, as do several of the ATTENDANTS.
         After some fencing, CINO *throws aside*
         his hood and cloak.

CINO.   A hood may hide a woman. This does
   not.
   Now, man to man!

SIMONE.   Hold on! You are not Dante.

CINO.   I never claimed to be.

SIMONE.   You acted him.

ATTENDANT (*brandishing his sword*).
   His false hood fits the falseness of his head.

Cino. If Dante's hood be covering my head,
  It does not cover all his head contained.
Attendant. It makes you take his place.
Cino.   What, I?
Simone.   Yes, you!—
  What else have you his cloak for?
Cino.   It was cold.
  I came here to Donati's niece,—to tell her
  Donati had returned, and then I felt
  A chill assail my back. This cloak has killed
    it.
  Is killing chills a crime you kill a man for?
Simone. But where is Dante?
Cino.   How should I know that?
Simone. He just was at the window here.
Cino.   Why I—
  'T was I talked there.
Simone.   Pretending to be Dante!
Cino. Pretending?—Now by all that makes me
    human
  Am I to blame that you have human nature?
  You work yourselves up to a fever, see
  The image of your own imagination,
  Then swear 't was I caused your delirium!
Simone. Humph! Leave him. Search the
    house.
      *Exeunt—Right—*Dino *and* Cino.

GEMMA (*confronting an* ATTENDANT, *as he turns
    from* CINO).   Nay, you forget
  I am Donati's niece.
ATTENDANT.   And what of that?
  This house is Dante's. You are Dante's
    wife.
SIMONE. He flies all colors and he follows
    none.
  So where they fly we all are sure to track
  A turncoat treacherous to every hue.
  Aha, he dreamed of ending factions here:
  He did it!—All unite in fighting him.
        *Exit—Right—*SIMONE *and* OTHERS.
Those remaining break windows and furniture.
        *Enter—Left—*DONATI.
GEMMA (*to* DONATI). What mean these crea-
    tures here creating chaos
  In this, my house?
DONATI. It is the house of Dante.
GEMMA (*showing him the deed given her by*
    DANTE). It is mine.
DONATI (*looking at the deed*). Aha! This makes
    a difference.
    (*to the soldiers.*) Hold, hold.
        *Enter—Right—*SIMONE.
SIMONE. The house has been searched through.
DONATI.   No Dante?

SIMONE.   No.

DONATI.   Withdraw, and set a double guard out-
    side.

    (*to* GEMMA.)

  They wrecked things badly.   Is there more of
    it?

GEMMA.   I have not seen.

DONATI.   Shall I go with you?

    *Enter—Right—*CINO *and* DINO.

                               Who

  Are these?

GEMMA.   Some friends of mine.   They just had
    come

To tell me they had heard of your return.

DONATI.   Humph, humph! (*to* SIMONE).   You
    give them passage.

    *Exeunt—Left—*SIMONE *and* ATTENDANTS.

DINO (*to* DONATI).   If you please,

We first would find our cloaks and hoods.

DONATI.   Of course.

    *Exeunt—Right—*DONATI *and* GEMMA.

DINO (*to* CINO, *collecting carefully, as he speaks,
    the parts of the torn manuscript in the
    wastebasket, and concealing them under his
    cloak.*)

    This world contains two kinds of people,
Cino,—

The kind who see the whole thing in its parts,
And those who see the parts, and not the
whole.[35]

CURTAIN.

ACT SIXTH.

SCENE: *The Interior of a large Hall in the Castle of the Marquis of Malaspina in Lunigiana. Backing, at the Center, are Curtains that can be drawn aside. Near the Curtains at the Left is a Writing Desk in which are manuscripts belonging to* DANTE. *Entrances through the Curtains at Back, and also at the Right and the Left.*
Enter—Right—DANTE.
Enter—Left—CINO.

DANTE (*taking* CINO'S *hands in his*). Why, why!—Thank God to see you once again!

CINO. I, too, thank God. How are you?

DANTE. Well enough
In body.

CINO. I am pleased to find you here
In such environment,—so beautiful!

DANTE. Earth might have more of beauty, had it had
More continence; nor spent, and spawned such crowds
Between ourselves and nature. As it is,
What tempt our taste appear too often served
Like viands one can scarcely find for flies,

Or test for spice and pepper.   Well, what news
From Florence?

CINO.   Could one call that news which but
Repeats the same old story?—brawls and mur-
ders?—

I had to fly myself.[36]

DANTE.   So had I heard.
But, thank the Lord, it soon will end now.

CINO.   Will?

DANTE. One time I trusted Rome—in vain.
At last,
Comes Henry of Luxemburg, the Emperor.[37]
Oh doubt, not him, a man of strength, have
seen him.

CINO. Beneath your cloak you seem to wear—
not so?—
A soldier's uniform?

DANTE.   I have enlisted,
And join him.   You come too—our very man!

CINO. All thought you firm of faith in the re-
public?

DANTE. I am. No tyrant ever triumphed yet
But first came cowards kneeling to be trod on.
Yet something more is true. Strong self-
control
Has never yet forsaken man or clan
Where did not enter the control of others.

Which others is the one sole question now
For half demented Florence.   Let a grip
So firm that all should feel it, rein and curb
And guide by reason her untamed disorder,
Think what our people, letters, art, might do.—
Why, all the world of thought would focus
   there,
And all enlightenment find there their sun!

CINO.   And you have waived the student for the
   soldier?

DANTE.   I tell you, friend, say what you may
   of thought,
Man's brawn was given him as well as brain,
And there are things to tramp for, things to
   clutch,
And days for doing.   They are brighter, too,
At times, than nights for dreaming.

CINO.   You forsake
The path of poetry?

DANTE.   Why no; not that;
Not wholly that!   I mean a man should wield
And welcome, too, the whole that nature gives
   him.
The fist is fashioned for the use of God
In just as true a sense as is the finger,—
What grasps a sword as that which guides a
   pen.

8

*Enter—Right—*ATTENDANT.

DANTE (*continues to* ATTENDANT).

  And are they ready?

ATTENDANT.   Nay, they will not go.

DANTE. Not go?—and wherefore not?

ATTENDANT.   Had you not heard?

DANTE. Heard what?

ATTENDANT.   About the Emperor?—was ill.

DANTE. Oh, yes; but only slightly—could receive us.

ATTENDANT. Nay, nay;—is very ill.

DANTE.   You cannot mean—
Impossible!—that he is dead?

ATTENDANT.   He is.

DANTE (*to* CINO). Now heaven defend! It must not, can not be.

ATTENDANT. And there has come a rumor with it too.

DANTE. What is it?—From your mien I should infer
It matters to myself.

ATTENDANT.   If you bide longer
Within this castle, there come hints of war.
A patron who should shield the Emperor's friend
Would seem to be the foe of Italy.

DANTE. Ah, so!—I must have time to think—
  I thank you.
          Exit—Right—ATTENDANT.
          (DANTE *continues to* CINO.)
          Oh Cino, Cino, did one ever dream
A fate like mine?—a civic leper, Cino!—
Turned out of his own home because a pest;
And then declared a pest to every home
That still would welcome him. This final
  blow,
It snaps the only staff remaining now
From which my soul could wave a single sig-
  nal.
Worse off am I, than were a soldier slain,
Ay, than a traveler in a tiger's den.
If but these limbs were plucked out, one by
  one,
I were not doomed to live on then alone,
An alien to all comrades, conscious ever
That to oppose the currents coursing round
Were vain as efforts of mere spurting spray
To still a surging ocean. Oh, my God!—
To live, yet be too frail to do the work
That makes a life worth living!
CINO.   I have heard
  You might go back to Florence.
DANTE.   How is that?—

Go back to Florence?—what?—and see those
    hills,
My home, my children, friends, and have a
    voice,
And be again a man with countrymen!—
Ah, say not that,—not if it be not true!
The brute-despair my soul has housed so long
Is trained to bear hard blows, and beat them
    back;
But this frail trembling babe of hope, just
    born,
Oh it were cruel murder, maiming it!

            *Enter—Left—*ATTENDANT.

ATTENDANT (*to* DANTE).   Some gentlemen with-
    out are waiting for you.
CINO.   They now may bring the hope I men-
    tioned.
DANTE.   Yes.

            He bows to the ATTENDANT.
            *Exit—Left—*ATTENDANT.

CINO (*to* DANTE).   Shall I retire?
DANTE (*gesturing toward the Right Entrance*).
                'T were well.   If seen with me,
My shadow might shed blackness on yourself.
CINO.   The blackest shadows fall from brightest
    forms.

            *Exit—Right—*CINO.

*Enter—Left—*ATTENDANT, SIMONE, *and* OTHER
DELEGATES.
All exchange bows.

DANTE (*to those entering*). You come from
   Florence, gentlemen?

SIMONE.   We do;
   And from your friends there.

DANTE.   Have I friends there?—Thank you.

SIMONE.   And they have thought it better for
      our peace,
   And for the peace of other cities near us,
   To end this feud between ourselves and you.

DANTE.   And I return?—What then are their
      conditions? [38]

SIMONE.   Confession, and repentance, and your
      fines,
   The stigma of oblation, and a robe
   Of penitence worn round the city.

DANTE.   Humph!—
   A fool's cap, too, like that which I am told
   Was worn by Lippus Lapi Ciolo?— [39]
   And what about my wife?—would like to
      watch
   Her Dante decorate a scene like that?

SIMONE.   She is Donati's niece.

DANTE.   If I return,
   I come as husband of Donati's niece?

And follower of his family and faction?—
Present my compliments, bid all have patience.
Not far away, a place is waiting those
Who wish to damn a soul for doing right,
In which that sort of thing is done much better.

SIMONE.   But—

DANTE.   No; there is no but.   God gives each man
One life where kindle feeling, thought, and will;—
And bids him hold it like a torch on high
To light himself and others.   Do you claim
That he should lower it?

SIMONE.   Why, in form, perhaps;
And forms of different shape hold torches.

DANTE.   None
Can ever plunge the torch beneath earth's mire
And keep it burning.   Yield in form you say?—
In form our frames but vehicle the truth;
Yet by its vehicle the world will rate it.
When comes the splendor of a monarch's march
Men cheer his chariot, not his character.
Should I let mine trail, broken, bruised, be-mired,
The world would hiss both car and occupant.

*Enter—Right—*ATTENDANT.

DANTE *pauses and bows to* ATTENDANT.

ATTENDANT. The Marquis comes. Perhaps
you would receive him.

DANTE. Yes. (*to* DELEGATES.) Pardon me.

*Exit—Right—*DANTE *and* ATTENDANT.

SIMONE. A game-cock crowing yet, eh?
But when they drive him from his present
dunghill,
He scarce will clap his wings with such a
whur.
No further need deceiving him, I take it!
None here will now oppose our seizing
him.

(*pointing to the writing desk, toward which sev-
eral* DELEGATES *move.*)
But first the desk, in it to find the list
Of Florence traitors, banded to uphold
The Emperor. Come their owner back, pro-
voke him,
And thus invoke the fiend in him to furnish
Excuses to offset the fiend in us.

*Enter—Right—*DANTE.

DANTE (*seeing the* DELEGATES *handling his papers*). What mean you?

SIMONE. We are gathering information.
A man so learned should encourage us.

DANTE. I thought that you were gentlemen
from Florence.

SIMONE. Yes, dealing with a traitor from Verona.

DANTE. Put back those papers.

SIMONE. When we strip your corpse,
And make your suit a sack to pack them in.

DANTE (*drawing his sword*). It will be wet
and heavy when you do,
And fewer of you left to carry it.

(DELEGATES *draw swords*.)

Enter—Right—the MARQUIS *with* ATTENDANTS
and CINO.

MARQUIS. Wait!—What is this?—You think we
dwell in Florence?
Or fail to furnish guests with knives to
carve
What leaves our larder?—You, forsooth, must
ply
Your own blades in each others' carcasses?

DANTE. They seized my papers, and would
seize my person.

MARQUIS (*to* SIMONE *and* OTHERS). Return
the papers, and return your persons
To your own city.

SIMONE. Pardon, we were told
This traitor would no longer be your guest.

MARQUIS. He is my guest, while here. I say
farewell.

(*He bows to* SIMONE *and* DELEGATES,
toward whom some of the ATTENDANTS
of the MARQUIS *move.*)

*Exeunt—Left—*SIMONE *and* DELEGATES, *followed by some of the* ATTENDANTS.

DANTE (*to* MARQUIS). No guest should be a
pest and peril to you.

MARQUIS. Nor I to him. Till you decide to
leave us,

You shall not lack protection.

DANTE. After that,

My soul will lack what more I need,—a friend.

MARQUIS. I wish to speak to you of that—
but later.

*Exeunt—Right—*MARQUIS *and* ATTENDANTS.

CINO (*to* DANTE). Where shall you go?

DANTE. Oh, high
up in the Alps,

Too high for anyone to follow me.

CINO. To be too high for that, you need no
Alps.

DANTE. Your phrase is kindly meant, my Cino,
yet

Conceive how barren, cold, and colorless

Is life upon the heights.

CINO.   Conceive, as well,
How far, and broad, and varied, and sublime
Are earth and heaven when these are seen from
    them.
Souls oft are driven from our lower life
That thus they may explore for us the higher.
DANTE.   You mean that when a man is bound,
    feet, limbs,
Trunk, head, he has no weapon left him save
His voice.   How well that I have kept these
    notes here!
    (*gesturing toward his desk*).
The slowest lines of thought are like the light-
    ning's
In this,—they never track the same trail twice.
Had these been lost, they had been lost forever.
CINO.   Your pardon, friend; nor deem it strange
    in me
That, when we met, my spirit's agitation
So wrenched the links of memory that they
    failed
To hold together that which chiefly joined
My journey hither and my thought of you.
    (*taking the objects mentioned from his
        pocket and presenting them to* DANTE.)
This miniature, Giotto's Beatrice,
His work and gift.

DANTE (*taking it from* CINO).

Oh, Cino, thank you, thank you.
How kind of him to send it!

CINO (*taking manuscripts from his pocket*).

These were rescued
By Dino Frescobaldi from your home
What time the mob made havoc of all else.[35]

DANTE (*taking and examining the manuscripts.*)

Why, Cino, do you know what you have
done?
That day, when, as you thought, my love ap-
peared,
She bade me write of what I just had dreamt.
While fresh in mind I sketched it, hued by all
The glory of imagination's dawn.
'T is here; nor since I lost it, head or heart
Has ventured to supply a substitute.
Yet, void of it, the path of thought I trod
Seemed like a day's where comes no sun.   But
now—

CINO.   Can mount, and, though none follow,
make all hear
Your voice come crying from the wilderness.[36]
You know, in ancient times, it was the poets,
Isaiah, Jeremiah, and Hosea,
Revealed the truth.   The priests could but
repeat it.

DANTE.   And now ours need their repertoire re-
    newed?
CINO.   They do; nor doubt that poets can renew
    it.
    Though no new message may inspire them, in-
    sight
    May often read through oldest form new mean-
    ing.
DANTE.   Ay, less the lack of truth makes mor-
    tals fools
    Than lack in thinking of the truth they have.
    One thing, at least, my Cino, life has taught
    me,—
    That reason's God must be a God of reason.
    If so, there lives no right but reason fashions;
    Nor is there aught that should seem right to
    man
    That fits not reasons fashioned by himself.
    So those who know they own an under-
    standing,
    And know how all things earthly join to train
    it,
    Yet think of God as all misunderstood,
    Must think with minds whose methods are the
    devil's.
    Pray heaven that we too join not in their
    error.

I oft have asked, my Cino, why it is
That all the world should hurl at one like me,
From state and church and home, what harms
    my life
Well nigh beyond what slew the martyr
    Stephen?—
Why must one live all buried save his voice?—
For nothing?—Nay; the paths of Providence
Were never plotted yet without some plan.
If God be one, his realm has unity;
And that quick blade of death, which cleaves
    the reins
And splits the wheels with which we race
    through life,
Is but a mystic wand beyond whose touch
A hidden life speeds on to reach the bar
Of everlasting justice. [40]   Where that waits
What need to prove? one merely needs to
    show,
From what life now is, what life shall become.
So I would do; and warn men not to take
Mere earth and sky for that one priceless
    jewel,
The soul, that they encase.   With gaze on it,
The men who keep their spirits clean and clear
From touch or taint of selfishness or vice,
May oft behold in depths of inner life

Which nearest lie to nature's inner life,
The image and the presence that reveal
The power and purposes that are divine.

   *Enter—Left—*ATTENDANT.

 (*He bows to* DANTE, *who returns the bow.*)

ATTENDANT (*gesturing toward* CINO).

 A stranger here would see the gentleman.

   *Exit—Left—*ATTENDANT.

CINO. Then "Au revoir," my Dante. Do you
  know,

 Your words recall what once our aged tutor,
 Latini, taught us?

DANTE.   What was that?

CINO.   Why, this,—

 A poet like a poem is a product.

Exit—Left—after shaking hands with DANTE,
  CINO.

  DANTE *looks toward* CINO, *as he leaves; then,
    taking from his pocket, where he has
    placed them, the miniature of Beatrice,
    and also the manuscripts brought him,
    and holding them in his hands, and gaz-
    ing at them fondly, he walks slowly to-
    ward the Curtains at the rear. He
    disappears behind them. A moment
    later, they separate, revealing the Closing
    Tableau.*

CLOSING TABLEAU.

*The Piazza di Santa Croce in Florence, Italy.
Backing is the Church of Santa Croce. In
front of it, on its Pedestal, is the great Statue
of* DANTE *as it now stands. If thought best,*
BEATRICE *and* OTHERS *may be grouped below
it.*

CURTAIN.

END OF THE DRAMA.

NOTES UPON DANTE

1 "When first the glorious lady of my mind was made
manifest to mine eyes, even she who was called Beatrice,
. . . she appeared to me at the beginning of her
ninth year almost, and I saw her almost at the end of
my ninth year. Her dress on that day was of a most
noble color, a subdued and goodly crimson, girded and
adorned in such a sort as best suited with her very
tender age. At that moment, I say most truly that the
spirit of life, which hath its dwelling in the secretest
chamber of the heart, began to tremble so violently that
the least pulses of my body shook therewith. . . .
In my boyhood I often went in search of her, and found
her so noble and praiseworthy that certainly of her
might have been said those words of the poet Homer,

'she seemed to me the daughter not of a mortal man but of God.'"—*Dante's La Vita Nuova, pp.* 23, 24, 26, *from the translation, as are all other of the following quotations from the same, of Dante Gabriel Rossetti.*

² "To the Florentine poets of this new school belonged . . . Dino Frescobaldi. . . . But the greatest of them are Guido Cavalcanti, Cino de' Sinibuldi da Pistoja, and, in his youthful poems, Dante himself."—*Federn's Dante and His Time, p.* 132.

³ "After the lapse of so many days that nine years exactly were completed since the above written appearance of this most gracious being, on the last of those days it happened that the same wonderful lady appeared to me dressed all in pure white between two gentle ladies. . . . She turned her eyes thither where I stood sorely abashed. . . . She saluted me with so virtuous a bearing that I seemed then and there to behold the very limits of blessedness. The hour of her most sweet salutation was exactly the ninth of that day; and because it was the first time that any words from her reached mine ears, I came into such sweetness that I parted thence as one intoxicated."—*La Vita Nuova, p.* 27.

⁴ "Of the poems contained in the book (*La Vita Nuova*) the first, as Dante himself informs us, was composed in his eighteenth year. . . . According to the custom of his time, he sent it to several poets, who answered it. Some of these answers are extant. Among them is a sonnet by Guido Cavalcanti."—*Federn's Dante and his Time, pp.* 204, 205.

⁵"It is interesting to read in Dino's book, who equally belonged to the White party, by what reasons, according to his opinion, influential Florentines had been decided to follow either party. Guido Cavalcanti had done so 'because he was a personal enemy of Corso Donati.'"—*Federn's Dante and His Time, p.* 172.

⁶"As I sat alone, I betook myself to draw the resemblance of an angel upon certain tablets. And while I did thus, chancing to turn my head, I perceived that some were standing beside me to whom I should have given courteous welcome, and that they were observing what I did; also, I learned afterwards that they had been there a while before I perceived them."—*La Vita Nuova, p.* 135.

⁷"What time she made ready to salute me, the spirit of love destroying all other perceptions, thrust forth the feeble spirits of mine eyes, saying, 'Do homage unto your mistress,' and, putting itself in their place to obey; so that he who would might then have beheld Love, beholding the lids of mine eyes shake, And when this most gentle lady gave her salutation, Love . . . bred in me such an overpowering sweetness that my body, being all subjected thereto, remained many times helpless and passive."—*La Vita Nuova, pp.* 46, 47.

⁸"I was in a place whence mine eyes could behold their beatitude; and betwixt me and her, in a direct line, there sat another lady of a pleasant favor; who looked round at me many times, marveling at my continued gaze which seemed to have her for its object. And many perceived that she thus looked; so that, de-

9

parting hence, I heard it whispered after me, 'Look you to what a pass such a lady hath brought him'; and in saying this they named her who had been midway between the most gentle Beatrice and mine eyes. Therefore I was reassured, and knew that, for that day, my secret had not been become manifest. Then immediately it came into my mind that I might make use of this lady as a screen to the truth, and so well did I play my part that the most of those who had hitherto watched and wondered at me, now imagined they had found me out. By her means I kept my secret concealed so till some years were gone over; and, for my better security, I even made divers rhymes in her honor."—*La Vita Nuova, pp.* 33, 34.

⁹ "He (Cavalcanti) was married for political reasons. . . . Rossetti sees a tendency in him to mingle 'the perversity of a logician' with 'his amorous poetry.'"—*Ragg's Dante and His Italy, pp.* 270, 282. . . . "His father, Cavalcanti, was a notorious sceptic and materialist. . . . Guido, too, passed for a sceptic." —*Federn's Dante and His Time, p.* 199.

¹⁰ "Then, musing on what I had seen, I proposed to relate the same to many poets who were famous in that day; and, for that I had made myself in some sort the art of discoursing with rhyme, I resolved on making a sonnet. . . . I determined that I would make a grievous sonnet thereof the which I will write here, because it hath certain words in it whereof my lady was the immediate cause. These words I laid up with great gladness. . . . Wherefore having returned to the city I spake of, and considered thereof during cer-

tain days, I began a poem. . . . After I had re-
covered from my sickness, I bethought me to write
these things in rhyme; deeming it a lovely thing to be
known. . . . And to the end that this inward
strife which I had undergone might not be hidden from
all saving the miserable wretch who endured it, I
proposed to write a sonnet and to comprehend in it
this horrible condition. . . . And because I would
willingly have spoken to them, if it had not been for
discreetness, I made in my rhymes as though I had
spoken, and they had answered me. And thereof I
wrote two sonnets; in the first of which I addressed
them as I would fain have done; and in the second related their answer as though it had been spoken unto
myself."—*From Dante's own accounts in the Vita
Nuova of his method of accepting from his experiences
suggestions for his poems, pp.* 29, 35, 87, 95, 142.

[11] "To this sonnet I received many answers, convey-
ing many different opinions; of the which one was sent
by him whom I now call the first among my friends.
. . . And indeed it was when he learned that I was he
who had sent those rhymes to him, that our friendship
commenced" (The friend of whom Dante here speaks
was Guido Cavalcanti—Rossetti). *La Vita Nuova
p.* 31.

"The responsive sonnet breathes a spirit of encour-
agement and comfort; it is the elder poet taking the
younger by the hand and bidding him be of good cheer."
—*Ragg's Dante and His Italy, p.* 283.

[12] Seeing that the epistle I speak of is in Latin, it
belongeth not to mine undertaking; more especially

as I know that my chief friend, for whom I write this book, wished also that the whole of it should be in the vulgar tongue."—*La Vita Nuova, pp.* 123, 124.

13 "In the year 1289 Dante . . . took part in the battle of Campaldino where the Florentine Guelfs, 15,000 men strong, defeated the Ghibellines and the people of Arezzo. . . . Dante served . . . at the siege of the castle of Caprona . . . in August of the same year."—*Federn's Dante and His Time, pp.* 201, 202.

14 "When I behold Bacchina in a rage
    Just like a little lad I trembling stand
    Whose master tells him to hold out his hand.—
Cecco Angiolieri, another of Dante's literary friends who sings the praises of his rather shrewish lady-love, Bacchina."—*Ragg's Dante and His Italy, p.* 197.

15 "From that time forward, Love quite governed my soul. . . . I had nothing left for it but to do all his bidding continually . . . albeit her image . . . was yet of so perfect a quality that it never allowed me to be overruled by Love without the faithful counsel of reason whensoever such counsel was useful."—*La Vita Nuova, pp.* 25, 26.

16 "Cosmo Donati was the leader of the Blacks—'a knight after the fashion of the Roman Catiline, but more cruel than he, of noble blood and handsome appearance, a perfect orator with the finest manners, acutest mind and the very worst disposition,' that is Dino Compagni's description of him. The very

beginning of his career was a violence done to law, for he liberated a criminal of noble birth with armed force. In the battle of Campaldino, it was he who decided the victory by a cavalry attack which he had been forbidden under penalty of death, to make."—*Federn's Dante and His Time, pp.* 171, 172.

17 "In the year 1289, the one preceding the death of Beatrice, Dante served with the foremost cavalry in the great battle of Campaldino, . . . when the Florentines defeated the people of Arezzo."—*Introduction to Dante's Vita Nuova, by D. Rossetti.*

18 "It came into my mind that I might make use of this lady as a screen to the truth; and so well did I play my part that those who had hitherto watched and wondered at me, now imagined they had found me out. . . . I made her my surety in such sort that the matter was spoken of by many in terms scarcely courteous; through the which I had oftenwhiles many troublesome hours. And by this it happened (to wit, by this false and evil rumor which seemed to misfame me of vice) that she who was the destroyer of all evil and the queen of all good, coming where I was, denied me her most sweet salutation, in the which alone was my blessedness."—*La Vita Nuova, pp.* 33, 45.

19 "In her salutation alone was there any beatitude for me. . . . When, for the first time, this beatitude was denied me, I became possessed with such grief that, parting myself from others, I went into a lonely place to bathe the ground with most bitter tears." —*La Vita Nuova, p.* 47.

20 "This excellent lady came into such favor with all men that not only she herself was honored and commended, but through her companionship honor and commendation came unto others. . . . When she drew near unto any, so much truth and simplicity entered into his heart . . . she showed herself so gentle and so full of all perfection, that she bred in those who looked upon her a soothing quiet beyond any speech."—*La Vita Nuova, pp.* 115, 112, 113.

21 "I, as was my friend's pleasure, resolved to stand with him and do honor to those ladies. But soon as I had thus resolved, I began to feel a faintness and a throbbing at my left side, which soon took possession of my whole body. Whereupon . . . being fearful lest my trembling should be discerned of them, I lifted mine eyes to look on those ladies, and then first perceived among them the excellent Beatrice. And when I perceived her, all my senses were overpowered, by the great lordship that love obtained, finding himself so near . . . until nothing but the spirits of sight remained in me; and even these remained driven out of their own instruments."—*La Vita Nuova, p.* 59.

22 "I received the visit of a friend whom I counted as second unto me in the degrees of friendship (Cino) and who, moreover, had been united by the nearest kindred to that most gracious creature. And when we had a little spoken together, he began to solicit me that I should write somewhat in memory of a lady who had died; and he disguised his speech so as to seem to be speaking of another who was but lately dead; wherefore, I,

perceiving that his speech was of none other than that blessed one herself, told him that it should be done as he required."—*La Vita Nuova, p.* 130.

²³ "After this most gracious creature had gone out from among us, the whole city came to be, as it were, widowed and despoiled of all its dignity."—*La Vita Nuova, p.* 123.

²⁴ "Then having sat for some space sorely in thought because of the time that was now past, I was so filled with dolorous imaginings that it became outwardly manifest in mine altered countenance. Whereupon feeling this, and being in dread lest any should have seen me, I lifted mine eyes to look; and then perceived a young and very beautiful lady. . . . It happened after this that, whenever I was seen of this lady, she became pale and of a piteous countenance, as though it had been with love; whereby she remembered me many times of my own most noble lady who was wont to be of a like paleness."—*La Vita Nuova, pp.* 138, 140.

²⁵ "At length by the constant sight of this lady, mine eyes began to be gladdened overmuch with her company, through which many times I had unrest and rebuked myself as a base person; also many times I cursed the unsteadfastness of mine eyes."—*La Vita Nuova, pp.* 141, 142.

²⁶ "The Pope by secret understanding with the Blacks sent the French Prince, Charles of Valois, as 'pacificator' to Florence. 'He came with the lance of Judas,' Dante says."—*Federn's Dante and His Time, p.* 245.

²⁷ "Dante was no longer a religious pilgrim but a political ambassador. 'Why are you Florentines so obstinate?' said the Pope. . . . 'Go back, two of you,' he said, 'and they shall have my benediction if they procure that my will be obeyed.' . . . Two to go, and one to stay. . . . Which of the three shall it be? Boniface had seen Dante face to face; here was the man who might thwart him. Better to keep this one in honorable imprisonment till the thing should be over and done. Was it not during these months when he was forced into unsympathetic intimacy with the inner life of St. Peter's . . . that he acquired that fine scorn of the venal and simoniacal Roma Cura which made him declare, in after years, that during this very year of Jubilee his exile was being planned in the place where all day long they made merchandise of Christ."—*Ragg's Dante and His Italy, pp.* 32, 33.

²⁸ "Dante's own estimate of Cino is clear from the abundant references in the *Eloquentia* where Dante habitually speaks of himself as 'Cino's friend.' . . . The first and strongest bond of sympathy was that sympathy of mind and taste."—*Dante and His Italy; Ragg, pp.* 286, 287.

²⁹ "Witchcraft and necromacy were normal factors in daily life."—*Ragg's Dante and His Italy, p.* 144. "Divination and necromancy were largely resorted to in moments of crisis."—*Idem., p.* 143. "So great a hold had these mission preachers on the popular imagination, that a very general belief was entertained in their miraculous powers, and some of them had the

reputation of being able to raise the dead."—*Idem, pp.* 97, 98. "The Florentines whose reputation for wit was . . . great . . . on hearing that the Dominican John of Vicenza contemplated a visit to Florence . . . cried out in mock alarm: 'For heaven's sake don't let him come here. For we have heard that he raises the dead, and we are already so many that our city will scarcely hold us.'"—*Idem.*, *p.* 200.

³⁰ "After writing this sonnet, it was given unto me to behold a very wonderful vision, wherein I saw things which determined me that I would say nothing further of this most blessed one until such time as I could discourse more worthily concerning her. And to this end I labor all I can, as she well knoweth. Wherefore if it be his pleasure through whom is the life of all things, that my life continue with me a few years, it is my hope that I shall yet write concerning her what hath not before been written of any woman. After which may it seem good unto him who is the Master of Grace that my spirit should go hence to behold the glory of its lady; to wit, of that blessed Beatrice who now gazeth continually on his countenance *qui est omnia sæcula benedictus. Laus Deo*."—*The concluding paragraph of La Vita Nuova, p.* 159. "As he explains it, the heavenly powers by mediation of loving and friendly spirits had so decreed it that his soul should be shown the way through the metaphysical realms where he could see the terrible retribution of God's justice and be satisfied."—*Federn's Dante and His Time, p.* 269. From the accounts given, we must infer that Dante supposed himself to have had an external vision of Beatrice, clearly separated from that which

might be experienced in a mere dream: and that this vision made "through the mediation of loving and friendly spirits," was of such a character as to cause him to spend most of the rest of his life developing from his own imagination the general conception of justice underlying his great poem. The scene in Act Fourth of this drama represents a very common, if not the most common, way in which, in all ages, men have been led to suppose themselves to have had an external vision of one dead; as well as the most common way in which, having had it, the vision has induced them to develop the general thought which, at the time of having it, has controlled them. The fact that Dante, so frank with reference to every other experience related in *La Vita Nuova*, never explained the circumstances or character of this vision, is in exact accord with what we should expect from a wise man conscious of the possibilities of delusion and deception connected with an experience such as is depicted in the drama. He would not have risked the danger of being thought a consulter of sorcerers, many of whom in those times were disreputable violators of the law, or of being thought a dupe of a monk of the church, following their practices in a supposed more legitimate way. At the same time, in the circumstances, notwithstanding much that could not absolutely convince himself, much less others, it is perfectly conceivable that the poet's sympathetic and imaginative nature should have been so profoundly influenced by the possibilities suggested by what he had experienced that this should have had a formative effect upon his whole career.—*The Author.*

[31] "The sight of this lady brought me into so un-

wonted a condition that I often thought of her as one too dear to me; and I began to consider her thus. . . . Perhaps it was Love himself who set her in my path, so that my life might find peace. And there were times when I thought yet more fondly, until my heart consented unto its reasoning. But, when it had so consented, my thought would often turn round upon me as moved by reason and cause me to say within myself, 'What hope is this which would console me after so base a fashion?'"—*La Vita Nuova, p.* 144. "Boccaccio tells us that Dante was married to Gemma Donati about a year after the death of Beatrice. Can Gemma then be the 'lady' . . . his love for whom Dante so condemns?"—*Rossetti's note on the preceding passage.*

32 "At the burial of a lady of the Frescobaldi family, a man's movements that had been misunderstood, had caused bloodshed. . . . In the year 1300, while Dante was one of the priors, they made an attempt to insure peace by banishing the most unruly chiefs of both parties. Among the exiled blacks was Corso Donati, while Dante, with his severe sense of justice, had suffered his friend Cavalcanti to be confined at Sarzana, where he fell ill from the unhealthy climate, and died . . two months later."—*Federn's Dante and His Time, p.* 240. " 'This unhappy Priorate,' he once said, 'was the cause of all my misfortune.'"— *Idem., p.* 240.

33 "Dante at this time contracted such enormous debts that many years later the family saw itself

constrained to sell estates to pay them."—*Federn's Dante and His Time, p.* 239.

[34] "The decree against Dante which to this day may be read in the so-called Libro del Chiode in the archive of Florence. . . . Dante and four others are condemned for peculation, fraud, extortion, bribery, and rebellion against the Pope and Charles . . . as proof, public fame is alleged. . . . Having failed to appear in court, all the accused in it were declared outlaws and exiles in perpetuity, and if ever one of them should be caught on Florence soil he should be burned alive."—*Federn's Dante and His Time, pp.* 246, 247.

[35] "Then there is Dino Frescobaldi, 'famous rhymer of Florence,' through whom, if Boccaccio is to be trusted, Dante received back in exile the original draft of the first seven cantos of the Inferno."—*Ragg's Dante and His Italy, p.* 273. "They had been left behind, with everything else, in Florence. . . . hurriedly concealed . . . when he was exiled. . . . And with the manuscript, says Boccaccio, came a fervent letter to the Marquis . . . urging him to persuade Dante to continue so great a work. And so, at the urgent plea of his host Dante was induced to proceed. . . . And for this good advice of the Malaspina Dante was so grateful, says Benvenuto, that he could never say anything good enough of the family."—*Idem., pp.* 332, 333.

[36] "Cino . . was exiled . . five years after Dante had been cast out of Florence, in 1307, the mem-

orable year of the advent of Henry VII.   . . .   One
of Cino's poems deserves the lasting approbation of
posterity, for in it he urges Dante to continue his great
poem and so redeem the pledge given at the end of the
Vita Nuova."—*Ragg's Dante and His Italy, pp.* 286, 287.

[37] "In the year 1310, Henry of Luxemburg came to
Italy.   By no one was he saluted with such exultation
as by Dante.   He wrote letters full of wild and trium-
phant joy to Rome and Florence and to all princes of
Italy.   He had an audience with the Emperor; and in
his letters he calls him the 'new Moses' and 'the Lamb
of God.'   He was full of the most ardent hopes . . .
but the enterprise failed, and the Emperor died at
Buonconvento on August 24, 1312. . · .   What
Dante felt at this blow he never expressed.   Now all
was over, all hope gone forever. . . .   Again he
wandered a banished fugitive on unknown ways."—
Federn's Dante and His Time, p. 262.

[38] "This then has been signified to me through the
letters . . . of several friends that if I were willing
to pay a certain sum of money and submit to the stigma
of being offered up as a sin-offering, I might be pardoned
and return at once. . . .   Far from a man . . .
be the reckless humility of a heart of dirt that would
allow him like a certain Cioli . . . to make an
offering of himself, as if he were a caitiff. . . .   If
any other way can be discerned which does not touch
the fame of Dante and his honor, that I will accept
with alacrity.   But if by no such way, Florence is to
be entered, then Florence I shall never enter."—*Letter*

of Dante tr. on page 127 *of A Handbook to Dante by Thomas Davidson.*

[39] "Some suppose the individual in question to be a certain Lippo Lapi Cioli, who among others is said to have been allowed to return to Florence in 1316 on condition that he should walk behind the Carroccio with a fool's cap on his head, etc."—*Dictionary of Proper Names, etc., in the Works of Dante by Paget Trynbee.*

[40] "Already at the time when Beatrice had been lost to him, and his thoughts followed her into the other world, his mind was deeply and intensely occupied with the Invisible, and his imagination attracted by its glories and hidden terrors . . . His eye pierced through the boundaries of time and space into the surrounding sphere of eternity; the wrongs done here were repaired and punished there. To see this, it had become necessary or, as he explains it, the heavenly power by mediation of loving and friendly spirits had so decreed that his soul should be shown the way through the metaphysical realms where he could see the terrible retribution of God's justice and be satisfied. . . . The state of horrible crime on earth was not all—the last word was not spoken here—he could be calmer and endure all knowing what was to follow."— *Federn's Dante and His Time, pp.* 268, 269.

MOUNTAINS ABOUT WILLIAMSTOWN

GREYLOCK.

FRIEND of my youth, my first of mountain
    friends,
Friend long before I saw thee, in the days
When, dwelling in a realm of endless plains,
Those whom thy shade had haunted pointed
    out
The clouds, and bade me find thine image
    there,—
With what delight my heart first welcomed
    thee!
And then, like one whose form lies prone in
    sleep,
My young imagination woke and rose
And strove to climb, and heaven alone can
    tell
How wisely has been climbing ever since.
With what delight, day after day, for years,
My eyes would watch thee looming through
    the light
Of early morn, and how they since have longed
For thee when absent! Nor, at any time—

Not after years had parted us—did not
The sight of thee outdo all expectation.

The works of human art may lose their charm.
The picture, statue, building, wear no mail
That can resist the subtle shafts of time.
Their brighest color fades, their bronze corrodes,
Their carving crumbles, and their marble
    falls.
Oft, too, when one has wandered far from
    home,
And craves the things he once thought wrought
    so well,
The soul's enlargement of the treasures missed
That each may fit a niche of larger longing
Will make all seem, when seen again, but
    small,
And, tested by the touch of present fact,
But fabrics of a dream conjured by fancy.
Not so with works of Nature. Years that pass
May make the field more brilliant with more
    flowers,
The ore more precious and the cave more vast,
And every mount, at our renewed return,
Soar higher like thick smoke above a flame
Fanned into ardor by the panting breath
Of fleet-sped winds that rush to its embrace.

And so with thee, O Greylock! Thou art yet
More grand, more beautiful, than when, of yore,
I sought thee, in that earliest rash attempt
To climb thy hights by scaling first the steeps
Of Prospect, pulled through thorny under-
    brush
From limb to limb, like some primeval man
When mounting rounds of some Ygdrasil tree;
Or when I tried that long, but shorter, course
That first essays Bald Mountain; or, again,
Sought first the Notch. To-day, as always
    comes
That sense of restful triumph when one nears
Those overshadowing forests that emboss
That glorious bowl, the Hopper!—when one
    treads
Those winding paths amid thick arching trees
Where, in the lack of outlook, naught can solve
The mystery of the hight save lungs that breathe
The thrill and uplift of a purer air;
And where, like spirits that have been inspired
But never can be conscious how or when,
Keen thoughts will still outpace achievement,
    till,
All suddenly, upon the eye will burst
The unobstructed vision from thy peak,—
The hills that sweep from Adams at thy base

To far Monadnock and the emulous mounts
That rise, as if from crowds that would be
    counted,
Above the hardly hid Connecticut.

Oh, some may praise the plain! It has its use
For plow and reaper, railway and canal;
But all that human hand could ever plant
Or thought invent, or energy transport
Could never, through long ages, bring to-
    gether
What here were gathered in a few short hours,—
A wealth of mound and meadow to suffice
For many a county, all rolled up in one,
A hundred miles of surface in a score,
A score of climates in a single mile,
And all the treasury of plant or rock
From half a continent arrayed against
The slopes that flank a solitary valley.
Who says there are no wiser views of life
Where every view displays a wider range?
More blest a decade spent in scenes like this
Than ages in some never-ending plain.

And what of those here who can never climb
These hights, or gaze upon their heaven-like
    vision?—

Did ever yet a form appear on earth
Divine in mission that would fail to bless
Those, too, who could but touch its garment's
    hem?
As long as thinking can be shaped by things,
And that which holds our life can mold our
    love,
What soul can seek the skies with wistful gaze
And be content with only soil below?
Oh, does it profit naught that one should dwell
Amid surroundings that no eyes can see
Save as they look above, no feet can leave,
To seek the outer world, save as they climb?
Where every prospect homes itself on high,
And each horizon seems a haunt of heaven?
One might believe, O Mount, as on thy sides
The thumb-marks of the Hopper show them-
    selves,
That thou wast made a handle, humpt and huge,
Which some magician of the sky could wield
While in the hollow basin at thy base
All things were lifted to a loftier life!

How blest the child whose thought begins to
    build
Ideals of deeds on dreams that, morn by morn,
Awake to greet a mother's flushing face

That bends above his cradle! Many a soul
Reared in these valleys where, like mighty
　　sides
Of some far grander cradle, lift these hills,
And where in bleakest wintry skies appears
Thy mountain's white brow warmed with flush
　　of dawn,
Has waked to see thee, day by day, until
The habit grew a part of life itself
And ruled his being,—that whatever light
Left heaven or lit the earth would find his form
In paths where it was always moving upward.

BERLIN MOUNTAIN.

THIS world is wider than the range of work,
　　Nor shows its worth through merely gar-
　　　　nered gains.
Yon barren mount where only scrub oaks grow
May yield, at times, a harvest for the soul
More rich than ever filled the fertilest farm.
Think not that every leaf that sprouts in spring
Must be a stem straight-pointed toward a
　　flower;
That every bud must bring a blossom-nest
In which to hatch and home a future fruit.

Full many a leaf can only catch the shower
And quench the dry limb's thirst; full many
    a bud
Grow bright alone as might a short-lived spark
Aglow to show some source of kindled fra-
    grance;—
Ay, ay, aglow to show itself a part and partner
Of that mysterious worship in which all
The worlds are joined, the while they hang on
    high
Like golden censers, hidden though they gleam,
And fill with sweetness heaven's dim dome
    above us.

In every sphere, beyond what merely meets
The first demand of need, there issues forth
A constant overflow. 'T is this that brings
More sunlight than the eye of toil exhausts,
More summer rain than clears and cools the air
Where smoke and flame the world's too heated
    axles.
'T is this regales the hunger of fatigue
By foretastes of refreshment never failing,
And shows, beyond the prisons of this earth,
Through opening gates, the free expanse of
    heaven.
Without this overflow, no wish could play,

No thought could dream, no fancy slip the links
Of logic, and wing off with childlike faith
And poise o'er mysteries too deep for sight.
Without it, not one poet would repeat
His empty echoes of life's humdrum work,
His rhythmic laughter of disburdened thought.
Without it, not one artist would essay
To mimic Nature when it molds to gems
Its melting worthlessness, or, like a wizard,
Waves with its wand to welcome bubbling
    froth
And turn to amber that which aimed for air.
Without it, ah, without it, there would be
No life of life more grand by far than all
That worlds can outline or that minds con-
    ceive,—
No wings to lift aloft our thrilling souls
And bear them on, unconscious how or why,
Far past all limits of all earth-moved thought
Until, at last, they seem to reach the verge
Of heaven's infinity.

                    Meantime, confined
Where only finite form can hint of what
Inspires formation, many souls there are—
Oh, may I join them!—who, in all things
    earthly,

Behold what evermore transfigures earth.
No scene can greet them but it brings to sight
Far less than to suggestion; not a tone
Whose harmony springs not from overtones;
And not a partial stir but, like a pulse,
It registers what heart-beat moves the whole.

So let this valley grow its flower and fruit.
So let the minds that fill the valley fare
On food they find in book and business.
Give me the flowerless leaf, the fruitless branch,
The mountain pushing up to barrenness,
The scrub-oak and the rock—and, oh, the view!
Away with work, and let me, free from care,
Mount on and up!—No weak distractions now;
No wait at Flora's Glen; no word to hint
Her modest welcome and her wanton wiles!
They seldom lured me in the past, and here—
Why, here, at present, look!—there lifts Bee
        Hill!
Come, serve with me, my day-long moun-
        taineer,
Our short apprenticeship, and compass this
Before the longer climb that waits beyond;—
Ay, like an archer when he tries his bow,
Essay this littler bend; and, by-and-by,
Our limbs will limber for the larger aim.

Now tramp we up the last vale's long ascent;
Now, on the narrow ridge, see half of earth,
And more than half of heaven, each side of
    us;
And here, upon the peak, at last, we pierce
The core where all sublimeness finds a center.
Not all, you say?—Then tell me where on
    earth
A lesser summit taps a larger view;—
See, south, the Berkshires, west of them, the
    Catskills,
Then, northward, up the far, wide Hudson
    valley,
The Adirondacks and the great Green range,
With, here and there, a knoll that gives a
    hint
Of highlands past the north Connecticut,
But, best of all, close by, the Housatonics,
And, walled against the east, this Greylock
    group
Heaped near like models to reveal in full
What wealth were in them all, if clearly seen.
One day like this that lifts a life on high
Where spirit seems to breathe its native air
Is better than to dream a score of nights
Where sleep is tinkering in its dark garage
The tire that gains mere physical repair.

And why should one descend?   Why cannot
   now
This whirling world whisk off the willing spirit
And let it shoot through space, and go and go,
And never come again?   Ah, why should fate
Leave thought entangled like an eagle here
Whose wings are bound, and feet can only
   crawl
So slowly, and, when one so longs to fly,
So painfully?—And yet there sounds a bell
From out the valley.   Why this call to work?
Why this reluctant journey down the hill?—
One scarcely dare look backward till, at last,
The autumn's gold and crimson in the aisle
That cleaves its glorious arch through Torrey's
   woods
Converts rebellious raving to remorse
That, even for an hour, one could forget
What beauty waits in low as well as high—
In all this realm, which nature, like a mother
That loves her child, has fashioned for his
   home.

Now back and down again to book and duty!
But who are these we meet?—Our comrades?
   —Oh,
Were they of us?—Alas, ye narrow souls,

Awake, and fly, like slaves that would be free!
Like those not made for soil but for the sky!
Bound down to petty tasks, more useless ye
Than ships loosed never from their anchorage,
Nor sailed to ports for which they have been
    freighted.
Oh, think ye ends that souls were made to gain
Were ever reached by one who never breathed
A higher air, or saw a higher sight
Than those on which contracted brows are bent
In library or laboratory?—what?—
Does thought grow broader, whittled down to
    point
At microscopic nuclei of dust,
As if the world were by, not with them, built?—
As if the game of true success were played
By matching parts whose wholes are curios?
Nay, nay! Life's greatest gain is life itself;
And life, though lived in matter, is not of it;
Not of the object that our aims pursue,
Not of the body that pursues it, not
Of all the world of which itself and us
Are parts. Nay, all things that the eye can
    see
Are but vague shadows of reality
Cast on a frail environment of cloud,—
But illustrations of a general trend

Which only has enduring entity,
And is, and was, and always must be, spirit.

There is one only mission fit for man,—
To be a spirit ministering to spirit.
What fits for this?—A breath of higher sky,
A sight of higher scenes, at times, a strife
To mount by means impossible as yet.
What then?—Believe me that the spirit-air,
Like all the air above the soil we tread,
Takes to its own environment of light
No growth to burst there into flower and fruit
That does not get some start, and root itself
Amid this lower world's deep, alien darkness,—
No spirit uses wings in heaven that never
Has learned of them, or longed for them, on
  earth.

———

WEST MOUNTAIN.

NO hands of human art could be the first
  To draw thy contour's broken lines against
The ended glory of the sunset sky.
No thought of human mind could ever plan,
Nor power uphold them.   Nay, they must have
  sprung
To shape like this when some primeval frost

Chilled, caught, and crystallized the storm-swept
    waves
Of chaos that, arrested in their rage,
They fitly might portray the power beneath.
Stay there, great billows, all your boulder-drops
Held harmless where they hang; and all the
    spray
That might have dashed above them merely
    leaves
Of bush and forest, held to equal pause
Save where, perchance, their fluttering, now
    and then,
Reveals a feeling that they once were free;
Stay there, suspended in the sky! But, sure
As days roll up the sun, an hour must come
When blazing blasts again shall shake these
    peaks,
Shall pile them higher, level them to plains,
Or melt them back to primal nothingness.
Meantime their mission shall be what it is:
To teach the world, not rest, but, restlessness,—
The aspiration and the aim of art
That will not bide contented till the law
Of thought shall supersede the law of things,
And that which in the midnight of this world
Is but a dream shall be fulfilled in days
Where there is no more matter, only mind,

And beauty, born of free imagination,
Shall wait but on the sovereignty of spirit.

How oft in youth I gazed upon these hights
Uprising to refresh a faltering faith
With wistful wonder and inspiring zest!
For this how often have I climbed these fields
From foot-hills to the Snow-hole; then, reclined
Against the western slope, looked off to give
A god-speed to the sun, and half believed
The blue-tint sky-sheet held to light against
The little town of learning that I loved
Could bear away with photographic art
That which should give enlightenment to all
The western land through which it should be
    trailed.

How often, with a single friend, at times,—
At times with many,—I have lingered there;
And then, as if the very air breathed in
From broader, grander spaces could inspire
To thoughts of broader reach and grander
    import,
It seemed that there was naught in earth or
    sky
Or shop or study—did we deign descend
To this more common world—that was not all

Discussed if not decided. Nor confined
To bounds material were we. While the wind
Would whistle through the trees and round the
    rocks,
Our shouts would join them, now, perchance,
    intent
To tempt the lonely echoes to applaud
Our strife to make our ungrown voices fit
To bear the burden of the larger thought
For which the world beyond our youth seemed
    waiting;
And now, perchance, though seldom recog-
    nized,
Nor if, though subtly recognized, confessed,
Intent to gain fore-echoes, as it were,
Of that which should be college approbation
When words that to the air were now rehearsed
Should load the breath that carries freight to
    spirit,
And, borne along the clogs of others' pulses,
Should start that subtle rhythm in the heart
That proves the presence and completes the
    work
Of what impels to rhythmic rhetoric.

Then, warned by coming twilight we would
    turn,

And dare to lose the path, and plunge adown
Where, lured by rock or rill, we snapt apart
The net-work of the tangled underbrush,
As if to seize wild prey enmeshed therein—
Oh, happy days of youth! when empty sport
Of mere imagination—fancied game—
Could fill the hunter's pouch to overflowing!
Ay, how much better than the days of age—
Alas, I fear it, too, of modern youth
For whom, so rich in matter, poor in mind,
We manufacture implements of play
That clip at fancies till they all fit facts,
Plane joys to toys, and level games to gain,
Till every pleasure palls that fails to pay
In scales that rate life's worth by what it
    weighs
When all the spirit's buoyancy is lost.

How often with no friend except myself—
And he, at times, no friend—my feet have trod
These woods, the while my soul has longed to
    rise
Successfully as field and cliff and tree
To hights where one could dwell above a world
Whose common life appeared but all too com-
    mon,
Its aims too low for love to seek and honor,

And yet a world in which my own self, too,
My body, spirit, all, bore part and share.

At times, these moods would pass like shadows
    trailed
Across the darkened meadows from far clouds
That swiftly sail the sky; at times, they came
To stay and root themselves like seeds that make
The brush more thorny with each season's
    growth.
And, oh, one night there was—can I forget it?
Not while the sky above and earth beneath
And all within my consciousness can last—
A night—and not the sole one—when, as if
My trembling human body were possessed
As by a demon of insane desire
To make its loneliness a fitting frame
For the deep loneliness of moods within,
I strolled, at midnight, through the shade-
    veiled elms,
Across the western rise, and down the hill.
What mattered how complained the creaking
    bridge,
Or bustling brook, disturbed by moon and me;
How marshalled into rows the ghost-like forms,
White mantled in the hill-side cemetery?—
On, on, I pressed until, through haunted aisles

Of phantom-fashioned trees and looming mounds
That rose like mighty tombs of giants dead
Whose spirits yet seemed round me,—on I
    pressed
Until I reached that great right angle where
All farms and all things fertile lie below
And only barren slopes of steril rock
And trees that nature struggles to disown
Await the climber who would still move on.
And then I paused, and then I looked below,
And asked what could be there for me, and then
I looked above and asked what could be there.
Mistakes of others and my own, as well,
The land's financial stress, and that strange
    stress
Of human fellowship which sometimes makes
A fellow-worker, from his very zeal
To help another, elbow him aside,
Had seemed to force me to a precipice
As real as any that my feet could find;
And I must fight, or fall; and if I fought
Must fight myself and fight my every friend.
Oh, do not think that heaven moves all alike!
Some minds are sighted for a single aim,
And right for others may be wrong for them!
Oh, do not think the tempter, when he comes,
Proclaims his presence through acknowledged ill!

His most seducing tones may leave the lips
Of friends, or those who best may pose as
    friends;
His direst pitfall-paths mount up, nor hint
What crumbling crags their garden glories
    wreathe.
You deem that, at the crisis of his life,
It was a devil Jacob wrestled with?—
Nay, nay; Hosea's term for him was angel.

What but my own good angel could recall
The plans of others and the hopes of self
For early, easy, individual gain,
Position, influence, all that most men wish?
And what except this angel's foe was it
That made contend with these a force conjured
From inward consciousness of mind and body,
With all the doubts that shadowed thought in
    one,
And nerves that stirred revulsion in the other,
As if to make my spirit fly as far
From fellow-spirits as those mountain hights
Were far from all that should be in one's home?

The darkest night brings dawn. You ask the
    end? —
What if the purpose that my soul then formed

Remain still far too sacred to reveal?
What if I failed to do as friends had hoped?
What if I lived for years discredited?—
God knows that I have tried to live my life;
Nor from the trophies of the outside world
Have often sought or longed for recompense.

Oh, there are views of life that so depend
On inward entity at work beneath
The whole that has been, or that can be,
    shown
In what men merely see or hear or clutch,
That each and all seem hollow as mere husks.
To-day a man is young, to-morrow, old;
To-day in health, to-morrow in disease;
To-day enthroned, to-morrow in his grave;
And not alone to man these changes come.
The earth, our home, that so enduring seems,
The sun and stars that light it from above
Belong but to a camp, set up to-day,
And, on the morrow, fell 'd and flung aside.

What then remains for life?—If one have aimed
For outward profit, nothing. If his thought
Have always, through the outer, sought the
    inner,
Then, not alone, the stars that shine on high

May all prove beacons, guiding on and on
To havens holding glories infinite,
But each frail flower that blooms for but an
    hour
May store in memory an ideal of beauty,
A sense of sweetness, that shall never leave
    him.

How vain to let affections all go forth
To things material, hard and heavy foes,
Whose mission is to fall at once and crush,
Or, through long labor, wear our spirits out!
How much more wise, behind the shape, to
    seek
The substance, and, in sympathy with it,
Learn of the life that never was created
But all things were created to reveal!
Ah, he who learns of this, and comes to live
In close communion with it, finds, at times,
When Nature whom he loves has laid aside
Her outer guise and clasps him to her heart,
That there are mysteries, not vague but clear,
Not formless but concrete, which, it must be,
That those alone can know, or have a right
To know, who always, like a faithful spouse,
Have kept their spirits to the spirit true.

And when these mounts, like mighty sheets
    above
Some slumbering giant soon to wake and walk,
Fall back to formlessness from whence they came,
What wisdom shall be proved the choice of him
Whose eyes, in mercy shielded from the blaze
On which the soul alone can look and live,
Did not mistake mere grossness in the form
For the true greatness of the inward force;
Whose mind too slightly taught, as yet, perhaps,
To read, beneath the picture, all the text,
Has yet surmised its meaning by that faith
Which, though its guide be instinct, dares to
    think,
And, though it bow to greet the symbol, yet
Lets not its magic cast a spell on sense!
To him the world seems but a transient school;
The universe, a university;
The blue that homes the sunlight and the stars,
A dome above a vast museum built
With glens for alcoves, plains for galleries,
And mounts for stairways, where he works
    and waits
Till comes the day he takes his last degree,
And then goes forth, and leaves these all be-
    hind,
Yet, in a true sense, holds them his forever.

PARALLELS AND PARABLES

THE LAST HOME-GATHERING.

THE age-worn dame her pale hand laid
    On the arm of her trembling age-worn
      maid.
"We both are white enough and lean
For ghosts to go with and be seen.
And I have dreamt they come to-day;
Thanksgiving Day they come, I say!
So get the table set," she cried.
"I will," her wondering maid replied.

Off through the wild November sky,
A storm, was it, that there drew nigh?
Or was it a pall-car of the dead
With crape-like curtains round it spread?
And oh, was a death-doom ever due
But lives that were sunny before it flew?
Heigh-ho, heigh-ho, as the thing came on,
To have seen the hurry and scurry, anon!
Heigh-ho, heigh-ho, to have seen the way
The breezes before it began to play!—
It came like a boy who whistles first
To warn of his form that shall on us burst,
As if nature feared to jar the heart
By joys too suddenly made to start.

It came like the peck on the blind by a bird
That taps for help when a hawk is heard;
It came like the shot of the pickets of rain
When sunshine flies from a window-pane.
But who of us ever can judge the way
A storm will strike from its first felt spray?
The walkers without soon found in the sleet
A net that was tripping their floundering feet,
A veil that was falling as light as lace
But snapped as it hit each stinging face,
Then shattered to scatter the street below
With hail-shot followed by smoke of snow.
The snow, it followed and lay like soot
Swept down from realms its white could pollute.
Or was it, instead, a pure rug spread
For the feet that came in that car of the dead?
The car moved on with threatening shade
To the home of the age-worn dame and maid.

Meantime, the table, it had to be spread.
"Get ready, get ready!" the white dame said.
"Get ready what?—We mortals eat.
But think you that ghosts deem eating a treat?—
No hollow within have they to fill,
No blood to flow, no nerve to thrill,
But get you flowers, all fresh and sweet,
A vase of flowers each guest to greet.

Of all things leaving the world at death,
There is nothing of which we know but breath.
And what but fragrance can they bear
The whole of whose bodies are merely air?"
So out of the hot-house flowers were brought,
And round the table wreaths were wrought,
And a full vase rose at each one's place,
Awaiting anon a ghostly face.
Beneath them all a pure white spread
Made whiter the light by each candle shed,
Each candle glittering, right or left,
Like a fire-fly caught in a June-night theft.
For a while, the flowers that warmed the room
Kept back the chill of the outer gloom.
For a while, the symbols of life and health
Had brought to that winter the summer's wealth.
For a while, those watchers had waived the truth
And brought their old age back to youth.

Then the door, it shook with a gust of the blast.
The ghostly guests were there at last.
"Come in, come in!" with eyes aflame,
"Come in, come in!" cried the age-worn dame.

"Ah, Bessie, my child, it is you! It is you!—
Still always the first, whatever you do?
How oft, like the dear, sweet elf of a dream,

Just mantling in light at the dawn's first gleam,
I have watched your form come shining through
A halo of rays less bright than you.
And when, with the others, you left for school
Your feet went always first, as a rule.
Your voice came first, when I heard their play,
And your voice first when they knelt to pray.
Of all our children you first were wed;.
And, alas, you too were the first with the dead.
Oh, lead you still amid spirits above?
If so, let me follow you there, my love;
For the one that led to the best things here
Must be some spirit that heaven holds dear.

"And Benny, my boy with the golden hair,
And a faith so sure that each day would be fair!
I think it was never a part of God's plan
That you should grow from a boy to a man.
So gentle, so yielding, your face all aglow
To follow each friend, and never say 'No,'
The skies too cloudless dawned for you,
Too sunny and warm—oh, nothing grew!
Your golden fields that we fondly saw
Were filled with a grainless crop of straw.
Ah, child of my heart, to think that the grave
Was the one thing left your honor to save!
And yet, a boy that so could love,—

Has a heart like yours no hold above?
If one's own spirit tempt not astray,
But only the senses it fails to sway,
Where worth is judged by spirit, I dream
That some prove better than here they seem.—
Besides, besides, with Bessie you stand—
Oh God, I thank thee!   She holds your hand.

"Here too comes Mary, you sweetest of all
That earth ever steeped in a brine of gall.
By your lover deceived, by many belied,
And long in suffering ere you died,—
Oh, what is the meaning of life like yours?
Does heaven mistake the traits that it cures? .
Or must the mood of a soul when trained
Be gauged by the discipline each has gained?
And is discipline never in reach of those
Whose natures have never been crushed by woes?
Do the cheeriest need the weariest strife,
Ere broken to bear what blesses our life?
Is the test of true metal the blow and the scrape
And the time that it takes to bend it in shape?
If so, perhaps, it is well that the best
Are those to whom earth brings the least of rest.

"And John, my eldest!—Are you too dead?—
No, no; I see—You are shaking your head;

And yet you have sent your spirit,—my stay,
As of old, when your father was taken away.
Of all our children, you promised the least,
Yet your rising above them has not yet ceased.
Your face was not fair, your mind not keen,
But you had what was better,—a strength
    unseen.
When all of our household shook at the blast,
Like a gnarled knit oak, you still stood fast.
No wonder the boy that so could stand
Is now a stay of our whole broad land!
Ah yes, though dense the depths around,
No high-aimed spirit to them is bound;
No heaven-aimed spirit abides in a grave;
But surely as air when plunged in a wave,
Whatever may try to hinder or stop,
There comes a time when it comes to the top.

"And Martha,—you always were planning for
    woe,
Yet whose whole life more joy could show?
In man as in nature, the outward jar
Less brings our trouble than what we are.
The wind may but tickle the grass or the tree
That lashes to fury the wave of the sea.
Your mood was a sea; but oh, how bright
It glimmered to image the whole world's light!

Your husband a model, your children all fair,
Your days your own, so empty of care,—
A life to which sorrow mostly came
Like a stranger of whom one hears but the
     name,—
Ah, well, it was kind of your spirit to stray
From your own bright home to see me to-day!

"And others too coming.—Oh how they crowd!—
Their father of whom we were all so proud,
My half, not only, the staff of my strife,
Whose loss could but make me a cripple for life;
And all the dear children of Martha and John,—
Our children that make our houses anon
Weird mirrors in which, with scarcely a blur,
Our own lost lives we see as we were.
Come in, come in, you are welcome, my dears!
Come in, come in, and forget the years!
Sit down, sit down! Thank God for the past
And life to be ours long as memories last."

She rose to greet them, but, fainting, fell—
Ah no; it was no mere fainting spell!
Her maid affrighted clutcht the dame's form,
And wept, and called, and heard but the storm.
A mighty blast the door flew back.
The lights were out; the room was black.

12

Her maid affrighted heard no more.
She knelt in darkness on the floor.

And when the neighbors came at dawn,
The table stood, the guests were gone.
And, side by side, at rest they laid
The age-worn mistress and her maid.

MIDNIGHT IN A CITY PARK.

S LEEP on, O World, that I no more shall see,
　　Sleep on, nor be disturbed by dreams of me.
What cares this oak for one leaf downward tost,
Or what all earth that one like me is lost?

The soul I love, the comrades of my strife,
All, all forsake me.   What remains for life?
Bend over me, ye grim boughs of the park,
And fold me in the coffin of the dark.

Hung high above this crape-like dusk of night,
The star-lights flicker, and, with star-like light,
The street-lamps ranged in order round me glow.
What victor's pall was ever lighted so?

Here let me end my life.   In death's long sleep
No more shall weary eyes close but to weep,

Nor thoughts keep mining from the darkened
    brain
Fit fuel for the morrow's burning pain.

I might have turned and crushed their power for
    wrong;
Have made them mourn for what they met with
    song;
I might have spoken out and proved the lie,
But meek, considerate, loyal, lo I die.

How many die, or all they live for lose
Because of weapons honor cannot use!
What hopes men bury that the ghosts which rise
May lead the dance of others toward the skies!

If but the truth of love a soul should tell
What hearts might break, what homes become
    a hell!
If touched by ardor of one's brightest aims,
How black his earth might scorch beside the
    flames!

There, in that mansion, where the light burns
    late,
A wife will smile to greet her drunkard-mate;
But, in her spirit, long for his fond eye
Who waits for her until that mate shall die.

Where, like a stable's, that low roof is hung,
Stern parents yoked and broke their loving
  young;
But love, if driven, is only driven away:
Thank God that lips tell not what hate might
  say.

Of yonder home a child was once the pride,
But floods of vileness whelmed her in their tide.
Diseased, disfigured, source of grief and shame,
She dwells there still, nor hears one word of
  blame.

And here where mourners watch a form so
  white
It scarcely veils the spirit's coming light,
Their aching smiles travest with joy-like arts
The throes of grief that rack their trembling
  hearts.

Who lives not conscious of some inward thought
Which out to outward life should not be
  brought?
How many a soul must purchase all its joy
With coin one test of ours could prove alloy!

Earth owes its faith to men who will not share
Distrust with him who now has none to bear.

No sighs of theirs give vent to inward strife,
Lest weak confession give it voice and life.

When comes a loss of fortune, honor, sway,
When threatens death that hope alone can
    stay,
When senile states presume they still have
    youth,—
Oh, what could curse men worse than words of
    truth?

The clerk, hard pressed, who holds the coffer's
    key,
The scribe in debt who writes that none can see,
The maid in want who fingers gem and dress,—
We trust them all for thoughts that all repress.

The forests flourish and the sweet flowers blow
Because of soil that hides foul roots below;
And all fair fruits of human life are grown
Above dark moods and motives never shown.

Ah, were they shown, did man not rule himself,
The world were whelmed in murder, vice, and
    pelf;
As vainly watchmen trod this dreamlike mist
As might some weird, unwaked somnambulist.

To wisdom's eyes all paths in life reveal
Each man a sentinel of all men's weal,
And often all their safety he must win
By first suppressing his first wish within.

Within himself when fierce the fight is waged,
Oh, who can aid the purpose thus engaged!
The soul, unheard, in darkness and alone,
Can never share a contest all its own.

None from another's practice gains in skill,
Or grows in power of feeling, thought, or will;
None with another goes to God in dreams
To seek the strength that his lost strength
        redeems.

What coward he, then, when the crisis nears
Who cries for comrades, nor dare face his fears!
No comrade's arm or mail can ever screen
The coming conqueror in that strife unseen.

All hail, dark Night, and darker Loneliness!
What whim was this that brought my wrong
        distress?
In life or death, knights crowned at heaven's
        high throne,
Pass up through paths where each must move
        alone.

Because, thus moving, many a brave soul
    bears
What none who else might be imperilled shares,
I hear the watchman's call, the midnight bell,
The city sleeps in peace, and all is well.

———

IDEALS THAT WERE.

I HAD longed for months to meet him;
   And then we sat, as of old,
When our days of life were dawning,
   With skies all red and gold.
But calmed was the thrill of his accent,
   And chilled the touch of his hand;
And under his lifted eyelid .
   No dear soul seemed to stand.

We talked of business ventures,
   Of losses, and gains ahead,
Of classmates,—a few successful,
   And some who had failed, or were dead.
But it all appeared like a story
   One read in a book long ago,
And recalls the reading to wonder
   How time could be wasted so.

We talked about women and marriage
　　And children, and how they grow,
That this one or that gives promise,
　　And others bring doubt, you know.
But our talk was the talk of strangers;
　　In touch with each other, thought I,
No more than a stone with a seraph
　　Asail in a cloud on high.

And then, at last, we had parted;
　　Nor had ventured one hint, forsooth,
Of the light that gave heaven its glory,
　　And earth its worth, in our youth.
He had wrought for wealth, I had married;
　　We had both earned board and bed;
But for what had we made a living
　　When all we had lived for was dead?

————

THE SAILOR'S CHOICE.

HE came to the deck at the call of the crew,
　　And had brought his violin;
So we hushed, as we all were wont to do,
　　And waited for him to begin.

A sailor-lad was he, rough in his mien,
But the look on his face, as he laid
His ear to the strings, I would rather have seen
Than have heard any tune ever played.

He stood like a picture painted in space,
And paused ere the bow he drew;
And then, that wonderful look on his face,
How deathly pale it grew!

"I am waiting the music the same as you,"
He said in a soft low voice;
"But between what we would and we would not do
We must make, at times, a choice."

He lowered the bow with a sad sweet smile,
"I think that the only pride
That I ever feel," he said, "is while
I am playing with you at my side.

"Yet I never seem playing for you alone,
For joining the voice of your call
Comes a voice more stern than a mortal's tone,
And it calls for my life, my all.

"It calls for my life. It draws my soul
Far out of me, while I play,
Till my body, deprived of my own control,
Seems only a demon's prey.

"He tells me then, with a frame bereft
　Of power to will or to think,
That for ills like mine no cure is left
　But the kind that comes from drink.

"You know my story,—too black to see,
　Too foul to paint or to tell,
All proofs or threats are lost on me;
　I rave as if earth were hell.

"Last night my blood-stained hands were torn
　From the throat of my own best friend;
And now, by the Lord, my soul hath sworn
　That a life like that shall end.

"There is only one thing that brings the foe
　That works this wrong within.
It is only music that maddens me so,—
　The music of this violin.

"How once I scrimped with all I could earn
　Till it I, at last, possest;
And how, when absent, my arms will yearn
　To feel it again at my breast!

"I tell it my pains, and its echoes come back
　So sweet I thank God they are there.
I tell it my joys, and the thrills that they lack
　My soul breathes in with the air.

"And now, no matter what fate I fear,
  No matter what ship I am in,
What comrade has left me, a friend is near,
  While by me is this violin.

"A friend! Oh, who but a fool would cling
  To a friend that can merely betray!
And yet to think so dear a thing
  Could have led my spirit astray!"

He spoke, and looked at it, then, on his
      knee,
  He broke it like one who raves.
The crew, to rescue it, sprang, but he
  Had hurled it off to the waves.

In the trough of the sea a moment it lay,
  And then came leaping back,
Like a living foe, but was caught away
  And lost in the vessel's track.

"I cared for it more than I think you knew"
  He said, with a sob in his voice,
"But between what we would and we would
      not do,
  We must make, at times, a choice."

AT THE PARTING OF THE WAYS.

DAY dawns, and just before my eye
   Two pathways fork the valley.
One turns to where late dreamers lie,
   And one where soldiers rally.
One slips by easy stages down;
   One climbs hights wild and steril.
One ends in luxuries of the town;
   And one in pain and peril.

Which make I mine?—Yon sluggard dreams
   His music of sweet slumber
To drum-beats of invading schemes
   Whose feet no man can number.
Despoiling good, enriching ill,
   These work where none suspect them,
And make mere slaves of thought and will
   That wake not to detect them.

Which make I mine?—On yonder hight
   Full oft, all ease denying,
One's only gain is conscious right,
   One's rest comes but from dying.
But once a prince here died to give
   His own good spirit to us;
And good for which we, too, would live
   May work less in than through us.

Oh, who would welcome not a strife
　　Where worth wins all its glory?
Nor waive the rôles of mortal life
　　For an immortal story?
The bugle calls the hill to storm.
　　My body thrills!—I use it
As due a spirit's uniform
　　Used best by those who lose it.

THE RELIGION OF RESCUE.

THE watch of the ship, "Lord Gough," called
　　out
　　Through the hurricane's howl, "A wreck!"
No shriek of the wind could have voiced that shout.
　　It brought all hands to the deck.

"No use in letting their signal fly
　　At half-mast"—muttered the mate;
"For heaven alone, in a sea so high,
　　Could save them now from their fate."

"That heaven be ours!" cried the captain brave;
　　"Ay, rate me worse than a whelp,
If, cowed by lashes of wind or of wave,
　　I dare not row to their help!"

Yet who of his crew would volunteer?—
　　Who risk their lives in the yawl?—
He looked where he thought that a few might
　　　　appear,
　　And found he could choose from all.

But wait!—On the mast of the floundering
　　　　ship
　　The flag no more could be seen.
The ropes hung loose that his crew let slip;
　　For what could the lowered flag mean?

Oh, could it have been but a false alarm?—
　　They all of them held their breath.
Could there be no need of an outstretched arm,
　　Or of rowing that race with death?

The captain probed with his eye-glass then;
　　"Nay, water-logged do they lie;
And, flying a flag or no flag, men,
　　We rescue them now, or they die."

He spoke, and his words, they rang like knell
　　On the drum of the outward ear;
But when on the inward soul they fell
　　Not a tremor they woke of fear.

Then soon, as a coffin falls to a grave,
  The yawl sank down, but alack!
Like fingers white the crests of the wave
  Were clutching and flinging it back.

Then, whirled, as it were, in a drunkard's
      dance,
  It staggered, anon, and lunged,
Then, tilted aside, like a hostile lance,
  At the hull of the wreck it plunged.

Three times, in vain, that helpless yawl
  Toward the deck of the wreck was tost.
Three times the wrecked, as it back would
      fall,
  Looked down with the look of the lost.

Then shouts came snapping like whips the blast.
  The yawl to the boom had clung;
And, one by one, from the wreck, at last,
  Black forms like bales were flung.

The last that leapt from the lone-left deck
  And called that the work was done,
Gave "Cleopatra" as name of the wreck,
  And the captain as "Pendleton."

"If you be the captain," greeted him then,
　　"In God's name, tell us, man, why
You lowered your flag, as we hove to you, when
　　You knew that you all would die?"

"We lowered it because our yawls were lost.
　　We could never have rowed to you;
And we feared that for you to come would cost
　　Far more than to us was due."

Then a low voice muttered, "When men would
　　　　find
　　Such a man as a man should be,—
A man that dares to die for his kind,
　　Then let them look to the sea.

"Whatever your churches or priests may claim,
　　When making their worldly rolls,
Those made by God for heaven will name
　　The men that have Christlike souls."

AFTER THE LYNCHING.

"WAIT, wait! I beg you wait!" I heard.
　　　　"I know you, yes,"—and at the word,
My arm was clutched; and, standing still,
I waited there against my will.

Amid the darkness of the night,
Two star-like eyes, a gown-cloud white,
And, just above, like phantom rays,
Gray, bony fingers met my gaze.

What skeleton had sought my side?—
"In God's name who are you?" I cried;
And, wind-like came a ghostly hiss,
"In God's name, let me tell you this.

"Someone did something wrong,—a man.
Some thought his color dark.   He ran.
We heard a tread, a hoot, a song.
What of it?—We had done no wrong!

"We never dreamed of their attack,
For we, we were not very black;
And should we flee, someone might say
That we were guilty—better stay!

"But they—O God, that hearts and minds
Should rave like brutes that color blinds,
Should feel no pity, weigh no proof,
But vaunt the rule of horn and hoof!

"They dragged my father from his bed.
They stripped and whipped, and burned him dead.
My mother, she bewailed his death.
They choked and wrung from her her breath.

13

"I ran, they followed.   Oh, the slough,
The brush, the briar I stumbled through!
And each time that I rose, I said:
'My God, why was I not born dead?'

"'Oh, why should He have made me so
That half the world must hound me? Oh,
Why curse the blackness of my skin,
And not their souls all black within?

"'Were all heaven's whiter, brighter fires
Burned out before it made my sires?
Ay, was there nothing left but soot
For men to trample underfoot?'"

"Too sad your lot," I sighed, "my child.
I wonder not your words are wild;
But nay; not all men hound your race,
Or deem it fills a useless place.

"No place in life but fills a need.
Who tills the soil, he starts the seed;
And on his kind of toil below
Depends the kind of fruits that grow."

"That grow!" she moaned; "they never will,
On sprouts that men so tramp and kill.
God grant they never live to see
The wilderness their world will be."

"God grant it, child," I said, and thought
How apt the message was she brought.
Her people might seem injured worse,
But mine had borne the deeper curse.

No pride in man can thrill the mind
That treats, like soulless brutes, its kind;
No heavenly father seems to cheer
Those who see not his children here.

The only joy that love can know
Dwells in our own hearts when aglow.
The only hope that faith can feel
Our spirits in themselves reveal.

"Hark, hark!" she cried, and through the dark,
As if the wind had whirled a spark—
Oh, would it kindle soon a fire?—
I saw her eyes flash past the briar.

Then I, too, heard those coming feet
And groans as of a wounded street.
Then I, too, ran with trampings loud,
And far from her I led that crowd.

I circled round it, came behind;
And then I cried, "Oh, fools and blind!
Who, who that once brute-force enthrone
O'er others' rights can save their own?"

RIGHTING A WRONG.

YOU think you will go now?—that I must be
     tired?—
   And go without John who brought us?—Why,
     why!—
Sit down here, and tell me what is it that
     fired,
   And is trying to quench, too, that flash in
     your eye.

Not pleasant, was John?—Did not wish you to
     dance?—
   How strange!—Just now he was here to tell
Of your triumphs; and pride, too, there was in
     his glance
   When he pointed you out as the ball-room's
     belle.

Oh!—only one man of whom you have heard
   That he wanted you not to dance with!—I
     see;
And that man a stranger; but you, you pre-
     ferred
   The stranger to John—which he thought
     should not be?

You say that women know best what men
    are?—
  And that men that are jealous are always
    unjust?—
What of that?—It applies not to John, so far;
  For he has a head and a heart we all trust.

Wait here, dear. You thought I was lonely;
    but no:
  Old age has pleasures that youth cannot own.
There are persons and scenes crowd the memory
    so,
    'T is a wonder we ever feel wholly alone.

You young people deem only you dance here.
  Why, dear, while you were there on the
    floor,
My soul, as it has not for many a year,
  Has been dancing one dance that I dance ever-
    more.

And dimly, yet clearly, I saw, too, to-night
  The man whom then I was dancing beside,
My heart all aglow, and my hope so bright,
  For I, I had promised to be his bride.

But into that ball-room, a stranger came.
   He looked like a prince as he followed my
      train.
His whisper was warm, and his eyes were aflame;
  And I was a moth, and was young, and vain.

Then he that I loved drew me off, and declared
   That this man was a knave, as he knew;
And I must not—but I was no child to be scared
   By one who was jealous.—I felt like you.

It seemed the crown-time of my life, that night.
   I was queen of all hearts, the beauty, the belle.
I sat on a throne in a halo of light;
   But my lover—he lingered outside of my spell.

He wrote then a letter. "What weakness!" I
   cried;
  "To be punished, his heart should be placed
    on a rack."
So all of his letters together I tied,
   And returned them, and waited.   They never
    came back.

He never came near me after that, dear;
   Merely dropped a brief line to say I was free.
He thought I distrusted him,—that was clear;
   And love without faith, he felt could not be.

The best hearts often, I think, are like his.
  They open their holy of holies within;
And that which profanes all, whatever it is,
  They cast out forever, as heaven would sin.

And I?—you have heard—it is not untrue,—
  That some love but once. Ever since that
      ball
I have loved no other my whole life through;
  And am only your old-maid-aunt, that is all.

What?—tears?—Not for me?—You awoke me,
      in truth,
  From the sweetest of dreams.—Can you
      guess what one?—
I am told that you look as I looked in my youth;
  And this John is his image—yes, dear, his own
      son.

He is coming again!—He is coming, you see!—
  And who was that stranger that talked to her
      so?—
She thinks you disliked him as much as did
      she.
  Keep him off! Girls feel it so rude to say
      "No."

Au revoir!—and now I go back to my dream.
  Some souls have missions because misled.
I must save her from dreaming how life might
      seem
    Were all that one cares for in life not dead.

———

SHE WONDERS WHY.

HIS form was manly, his face was fair,
    His character true and pure.
Would she be his bride?—He lingered there;
  But "Nay," she said; he was "poor."
She sits alone, and wonders why
He should think with nothing a bride to buy.

He flung to the war the form she had spurned;
    He hurled it far in the strife.
His brave assault had a victory earned;
    But he, he had lost his life.
She sits alone and wonders why
A man who loved her should need to die.

They brought him home, and buried him deep,
    In a soldier's raiment clad;
And she, she came to see and weep;
    For his life had seemed so sad.

She sits alone, and wonders why
No lover comes as the years go by.

THE WALL–FLOWER.

OUTSIDE the whirlpool of the ball,
    A stranded flower against the wall,
She blusht to feel she stood too tall
    For aught about to hide.
Why should a soul to earth be brought
And framed within a form, she thought,
That shows no beauty to be sought?
    And deeply sad, she sighed.

A strong man of the world was he,
And round about him rusht that sea
And swept him off; but not to be
    The end of all his care.
So held in hands and tript in trains,
He did not lightly wear the reins,
But seemed a spirit dragged in chains;
    Then saw her standing there.

He stood beside her soon, and talked,
And out the garden door they stalked,
And where the boughs were thick they walked,
    Ah, how the hours had flown!

She never heard a man before
With such a stock of soulful lore,
Nor thought to meet his equal more;
    Nor felt again alone!

HOMELESS.

" PERHAPS I failed in thrift, of old.
    It may serve me right to be hungry and cold;
But why should my babe, so frail, so fair,
Be left with nothing to eat or wear?
Come, come, my child, out there on the street
Are beautiful homes with supper and heat;
And when they see to whom they can give,
Oh, then they will help thee and let thee live."

She opened the door.   She walked the street.
She held to the passer her babe so sweet.
Up many a stately porch she crept;
But closed to her call their doors were kept;
And some there were even that named police,
Till she only dared to hold her peace.
Oh, beautiful homes, with so much to give,
Do none of you care that her child should live?

She sank on a seat.   They sat in a park.
One locked its gates.   The night grew dark.

The air was chilly.   The snow fell deep.
There was no one to bid her babe not weep.
There was no one to cover its form from the
    blast;
And yet, how quiet it slept at last!
Oh, beautiful homes, keep what ye might give.
None need care now that her child should live.

THE BLIZZARD.

WITH a scowling sky blue-black from a blow,
    And the whur of a giant in skirts of snow,
  The blizzard came howling ahead.
"O God," she cried," what a fearful sight!
And my children are coming from school, to-
    night!
  I must fetch them home," she said.

She tramped in the snow, and battled the blast,
And just had fainted, but saw, at last,
  The dear little pair that she sought.
"Thank God," she cried, and, with freezing tears
That fell like pearls, while she freed her fears,
  To her breast the two she brought.

The blizzard had gone, and the sun shone bright;
But under a snow-shroud—oh so white!—

The children and mother lay.
Thank God, she was there with a kiss and a word;
The deepest prayer of her heart had been
        heard;
    She had taken them home to stay.

IN THE LIFE BEYOND.

So pale is the little cheek
    And the still lips will not speak.
Oh, where is the life I seek,
        My child, my child?
Oh, why has the spirit flown
Without me to lead it, alone,
Out into the dark unknown,
        So wide, so wild?

Who now when dreams grow deep
Will watch at the gates of sleep,
Or wipe these eyes when they weep
        At scenes unkind?
Who now when wish and thought
So yearn to be helpt or taught
Will bring the boon they had sought,
        But could not find?

Oh, surely love must care
For child-life everywhere!
Kind hands, they must be there,
    So soft, so fond!
They must keep my child for me,
Forever a child to be,
Where forever a home I see
    In the life beyond.

SUGGESTIONS FROM CHURCH, STATE, AND SOCIETY.

A HYMN FOR ALL RELIGIONS.

OH Life that lives beyond desire
   In peace that makes the future blest,
Through each new death, oh lift us higher,
   Till all shall with the Bhudda rest.

Oh Mind that knows what all would know,
   Although Thyself be never known,
Hear us whose thought would not forego
   What wise Confucius made his own.

Oh King whose glories mortal saw
   When Moses near'd Mount Sinai's fires,
Hear us who still regard thy law,
   And serve the Lord who saved our sires.

Oh Leader who one prophet hath
   To guide the faithful soul to thee,
Hear us who ne'er forsake the path
   Wherein Mohammed's form we see.

Our Father from thy home above
　　Thy call was heard and it sufficed,
Hear us for him who proved thy love,
　　Hear us whose faith hath found the Christ.

FULL CHORUS.

Oh Thou that over all must reign,
We should Thy glorious throne profane,
Did we not walk in his dear shade
Whom Thou our light of life hast made.
Oh save us through his truth and grace,
Nor let the lightning of Thy face
Strike those who follow in his train.

RESPONSE.

Not every man that names the name
　　That is the Lord's can enter here;
But only those whose inward aim
　　Would do his will howe'er made clear.
For naught can reach the Spirit's throne
Save what in spirit spirits own.

THE AMERICAN PIONEER.[1]

O F all the world's grand heroes, none has won
   The right to be more honored or more dear
Than he who, traveling toward the setting
     sun,
   Became our country's western pioneer.
For strife that made our free land what it is
   Our debt is not to Pilgrim sires alone.
This later sire, too, that each heir of his
   Might weal inherit, oft gave up his own.

Think not for weakness that could not have
     wrung
   His due from rivals in his childhood's home,
He turned from scenes that he was reared among,
   And chose in lone untrodden wilds to roam.
The fledglings first to flap a restless wing
   Have calmed each mate that would their whir
     contest,
Long ere, at last, they take the fateful spring
   That bears them off forever from the nest.

[1] Read at the celebration of the hundredth anniversary of the founding, in 1803, of Potsdam, N. Y., and of St. Lawrence Academy, by Benjamin Raymond, Civil Engineer and County Judge.

And not for fame wrought he who moved away
   Where few could note his deeds or shout his
      name.
No throngs he drew to tempt him to display;
   No couriers flew his triumphs to proclaim.
For years no sound his pride of self increased.
   He heard but echoes of his axe and gun,
The night-howl of the wolves, or, when they
      ceased,
   The singing of the birds to greet the sun.

And not for coin he left the town's close ranks
   That, bartering, beat him in tight-fisted
      strife,—
Their plants all factories, their granaries banks,
   Their atmosphere but that of man-made life.
His mood preferred God's primitive exchange
   Where well tilled grain in grain gives back
      returns;
Nor did he ever deem it wrong or strange
   That rest enjoys no more than effort earns.

Nor fled he like some prodigal, to please
   Himself, and thus a father's purpose foil.
No seeker for a life of selfish ease
   Would so enroll with volunteers of toil.

He fought the wild beasts backward through the
 wood;
  To pave the swamp, he pried the ledges down;
Grubbed roots to clear the field for others'
 food;
  Felled trees with which his followers built the
 town.

He went as if some call within the soul
  Had come to urge him toward the untamed
 wild,—
A call that all his life-work should control,
  A father's call, of whom he seemed a child.
He must have felt that earth's unconscious
 growth
  Could flower alone in conscious deeds of man,
And where man wrought with nature, there that
 both
  Were working to fulfill a God-formed plan.

His body served the soil, but from the skies
  He breathed the spirit in with which he
 wrought.
In them he saw fair homes and cities rise;
  No facts could bury faith that lived in
 thought.

His life was hard, yet seemed a rare romance,
　　The sense in thrall, the soul at liberty;
And, winged beyond his age in its advance,
　　What he saw then, we now term prophecy.

Oh, would his children in this age were true
　　To that which they inherit from the past!
Would they could look beyond each present view
　　Up through the clouds and forward through
　　　　the blast!
Still waits for us that city which our sires
　　Saw looming in the realm of their ideal;
Still needs the world the spirit that aspires
　　To lead where earth is new and heaven seems
　　　　real.

————

GOD BLESS AMERICA.

GOD bless America, and still
　　Our nation's guardian be,
As when, of old, to work thy will,
　　Our fathers made it free.
We thank thee for our fertile fields,
　　For mines our high hills dome;
But more for kindly rule that yields
　　Its due to every home.

Oh, never, where brute-force would fight
   The ways humane it hates,
Could aught resist it like the might
United to uphold the right
   In these United States.

God bless "the Stars and Stripes" above
   The school, the shop, the farm.
To nothing worthy of man's love
   Its flying could do harm.
Let others boast a flag that waves
   In triumph where men kill,
We prize our own as one that saves
   From wrong that war would still,—
A symbol of just laws that lead
   To life that peace creates,
While men to men fair play concede,
And States lack neither help nor heed
   That are United States.

God bless the world by blessing here
   The land of equal rights.
The man who deems each man his peer
   No other's nation slights.
Ay, where no earthly lords enthrall
   Through faith in sword or throne,

In God we trust by trusting all
  In whom His traits are shown.
The largest hope since time began,
  For which the whole world waits,
Is that for which our statesmen plan,—
The coming Parliament of Man,
  The world's United States.

TO THE WIFE OF A PUBLIC MAN

AS REPORTED BY A MIND-READER.

YOU point toward us your finger.
    We press it, if we choose;
But, oh, we must not linger
    Your patience to abuse!

We dare your face to look at;
    But us you scarcely see.
Big fish for you to hook at
    Are not such fry as we.

Yet not to pay this visit
    Had seemed for us a slight.
It is not easy—is it?—
    For you to be polite.

Of course, we know your reason;
  It is so hard to drop,
Or in or out the season,
  The manners of the shop,—

The business-ways that culture
  New meanness, day by day,—
The swaggering of the vulture,
  The squirming of its prey.

Did you not show your heart set
  On those with gold to spend,
You might then to your smart-set
  Appear some poor man's friend.

You think, to be successful,
  With snobs you ought to score;
Yet those with purses less full,
  They number many more.

They vote the world's opinion;
  And when they see your mien,
Not one would seem a minion
  That you may seem a queen.

Not one thing can you boast of
　　That they would not dispute,
Save when you make the most of
　　What makes you most a brute.

Thank God, ours is a nation
　　That his own test controls ;
Nor bows before high station
　　When held by low-lived souls.

We deem it merely human
　　To not put under ban
The deference due each woman,
　　The honor due each man.

But you—from us you differ,
　　And does your husband, too?—
Or only for your sniffer
　　Must we bid him adieu?

When us he seeks applause of
　　And bids you join his trick,
Why spoil the show because of
　　Your mule-like itch to kick?

We knew your record shady,
But if that thriftless cot
Had turned you out a lady,
All this had been forgot.

But now—how deeds expose us!—
Your vulgar strain is real.
Your overbearing shows us
Your underbred ideal.

HER HAUGHTINESS.

SHE stands erect and overlooks
Those she would make look up to her;
And, scepter-like, her straight hand brooks
A touch, but not a hand-shake, sir.
She walks, and clearance for her feet
Expects from all men not profane.
No brute so trod a field of wheat
To bend and break, not thresh, the grain.

The poor and weak—oh, not to them
She turns a heedful eye or ear!
Could rags of theirs offset a gem?
Or feeble voices lend a cheer?

Yet if a great man you—aha!—
    Or wealth or honor can confer,
No Moses tapping Meribah
    Could slake conceit's hot thirst like her.

And would you question how was won
    The high regard she claims from earth?
Think not she feels that service done
    For manhood measures manhood's worth.
Nay, nay; no meanest epithet
    Her antecedents could traduce
Which one, save those who can forget,
    Or wealth can bribe, would deem abuse.

I say this not because no white
    Became her mother but the shroud's;—
A flower may blossom, sweet and bright,
    Though grown in mire where hang but clouds;
And not because, to dig for pelf,
    Her father soiled both soul and hand;—
Each spirit by and in itself,
    Insures what heaven should bless or brand.

I blame her not because her veins
    Contain her foul forefathers' blood,
But that her own work now maintains
    The present spring that taints its flood.

I blame the beauty in her face,
   The beacon-flashes in her eye,
The faultless form, the luring grace,
   All made by her a living lie.

A living lie!—In realms of right
   With no such charms is wrong indued;
All beauty is the halo bright,
   The coming glow of God and good.
What foe to worth that rules above
   Sent forth, to serve but greed and pelf,
This outward messenger of love
   With inward mission but for self?

In her the smile that brings life cheer,
   The tone that faith can understand,
The phrase that makes the doubtful clear,
   The clasp that plights the helping hand,
The sympathies that zest infuse,
   The comradeships that souls ally,
Her heart has never thrilled to use,
   Her head has never planned to try.

Alas, to know what life can be,
   And then to know what her life is!—
That, such a thing to pity, she
   Should dream of her priorities!

I doubt if one could find a soul
   Whose love for her would be avowed;
And yet, when playing such a rôle,
   Good God!—to think she can be proud!

THE SOCIETY LEADER.

No princess merely born to reign
   Could boast a more desired domain,—
More loyal followers in her train,
   For she rules head and heart.
To vie with her, the rolling drum,
The bugle call would both be dumb.
They could not bid such homage come
   Or such repute impart.

And not for naught do men, I ween,
Like bees that swarm, make one their queen,
And, actor-like in every scene,
   Yield her the leading rôle.
For if that rôle make true and real
The hope that heeds a high ideal,
What heaven-sent goddess could reveal
   More good to bless the soul?

But if her social touch infest
The town with some contagious pest,
Whose nights of fever know no rest,
   Nor days, in all the seven,
Her hand may guide where souls but weep,
Not less for loss of dreams in sleep
Than loss of waking dreams that keep
   The spirit near to heaven.

And if she lure to seek success
Through debt-bought houses, motors, dress,
And all that drugs to thoughtlessness
   The thought that minds would shirk,
Be dupes beguiled to fling away
The hard-earned token-coin of pay,
Dishonoring, in the craze of play,
   The law that blesses work,—

If thus to ill her lead incline,
Deluded throngs that push and pine
To get inside her circle's line
   Might better seek a herse.
No soul that once becomes the prey
Of her whose form exerts the sway
Of beauty but to lead astray
   Could find a devil worse.

LOVE AND LIFE.

LOVE AND LIFE.

I

LIFE is a mystery, mystery bound.
  Above or about us no rest is found.
Our past is a dream of the soul's dim home;
Our future a scheme for the mist and the foam.
The winds drive us on; we shudder but steer;
We tack for safety, we drift in fear;
We cry for help and a helper, but none
Will answer our cry; we struggle alone.
If our landing, indeed, were near some light
To signal the harbor were now in sight.
Be alert, my soul, nor ever a ray
Let gleam unused when the gloom gives way.
No doubt or danger can ever dispense
With a sigh or a sign for spirit or sense.

II

Ah, whither do lines of the long course tend,
And when will the task of tracking them end?

No voice can tell us.   No other can show
What no one except ourselves can know.
         On the way to the grave,
         Though, over the wave,
Loom many a shore past many a shoal,
But one port waits for any one soul.

By himself alone
   He must make his quest
For a home to own
   In the land of the best.

III.

What order but this,
   At the world's first dawn,
Made clear the abyss
   Through the dark withdrawn?
Off flew on their missions
   The systems and stars,
To waiting fruitions
   That time still bars;
And high rose the mountains;
   And broad reacht the plains;
And up burst the fountains;
   And down fell the rains;

And, water'd between,
Came on earth that was green;
    And, fragrant
    And beautiful,
       Herbage and flower;
    And, vagrant
      Or dutiful,
        Manhood, a power,
         Whose glory
         And story
       Is always this,—
     That the spirit of life
     Is a spirit of strife;
And, whatever the thing we may gain or miss,
The end of it all is to lie like a knight
Whose rest is the weariness won in a fight.
The world whirls us on, and, in reason or rage,
We bustle and jostle from childhood to age.

IV.

    Lo, feebly rises
      A voice that wails,
   As life surprises
      And lifts the veils
From the eyes of a babe that little prizes

An unsought birth
In a lone chill earth
Where it weeps and wonders what life is worth!
The eyes draw back from the points of the light
    That glance from a world that is all in a glitter.
The cheeks to mysteries huge look fright.
    The swaddling chafes and the cups are bitter.
The small hands clutch for motes of the air,
    For plaits of the dress, for folds of the bed;
But the marvels move and mingle and tear,
    Redoubled by every shred.
Soon, limbs that balance the tottering brain
Fall down in the pathway damp with the rain;
Or fly with shrieks from the boisterous joys,—
The barking and bounding of dogs and boys,
And wheels incessantly grinding out noise.
And if, indeed, the flowers be sweet,
The garden is close to the long, wide street,
And all the big houses, and who can they be
The smileless people so stern to see?

V.

The lone little being, bewildered by needs
And thoughts it can speak not, or nobody heeds,
Ah, where can it find any respite or rest,
Till cradled, anon, on its mother's breast,

Its faith a feeling by none withstood;
Its hope that of saints in God and in good;
And its love, ah would none ever could
    roam
From the LOVE OF THE CHILD in the joy of the
    home

> *Where none seem alone,*
> *But a part of life's whole,*
> *Whom love, when shown,*
> *Hath joined in soul.*

VI.

Behold, at the heart's least token,
    The babe and the mother,
Whose lives apart had broken,
    At one with each other!
But, ah, sweet babe, if thy mother incline
    To welcome thy fears
With words that direct toward the work of the
    years
More voiced for her nature than thine,
The first of earth's parents could no more
    undo
Than the last of their kind, through self-seeking
    too,
    Who tamper with nature's design.

VII.

What a spirit earth needs in the mother!
　Who else can inspire
To a life to be loved by another
　The future's desire?
The tender plant that springs to the air
　From the small frail urn of youth
Is trained, if at all, by a woman's care
　For the flowering and fruitage of truth.
Each home is an Eden that owns an Eve
Whose deeds make all life joy or grieve.

What a work to be done by the mother,
　Ere, out from the home,
To be shadowed and shaped by another,
　The child must roam;
Ere battered and tattered by earth,
　No matter how loath,
With a push that is his by birth,
　An impulse of growth,
He is warring to win or to lose in the strife
Where the stoutest of all must battle for life,

VIII.

　God shield his frame
　And straighten his aim;

For no help else, or early or late,
Can ward his form in the war with fate;
No help ward those who must weep for one
Who fell as the battle had just begun;
Whom life had afforded not one chance
To tender his aid in the world's advance.
Oh, if there be laws that faith can trust,
High laws that righten all things unjust,
What spheres for dreaming and doing must lie
In airs not domed by a mortal sky!
What fulness of living must life contain
Where losing one's life on earth seems gain!
Well might it seem so, if a soul no more
Should need to struggle, bruised and sore,—

By himself alone
  To make his quest
For a home to own
  In the land of the best.

IX.

What joy does the bell
  Of the school foretell
To the child who first, with book and slate,
And bounding step for his fancied fate,

Goes out from home, whose dear eyes yearn,
Out into the world with a world to learn!
　Alas for the feet that trip through the street!
　　　　Those throngs before
　　　　The school-house door
　Are a hostile host to meet.
Those unknown quizzical girls and boys
　　　　Have made the eye
　　　　So keen, grow shy;
　And a blush takes the place
　Of the flush on the face
That shrinks from the hoped-for joys;
And sad to the stranger and drear and dim
Seems a world of pleasure that knows not
　　　him.

X.

　What zest does the sport
　Of the school import
Into life, as its ways unfold!
As the child in his turn grows bold;
And, with tests that have made his own soul
　　　stout,
Assails his fellows their fears to rout!
Alas for his elders' rebukes and sighs!

His mind is away
    At play all day,
Nor cares for a school-room prize.
But if a spirit of love and of zeal
    In others inspire him
    Through toils that tire him,
    What nobler throne
    Could their spirits own,
What realm more royal in weal!
The autocrat's pride in his haughtier train
The miser's clutch for the glut of his gain,
    Are as shade to the light,
Are as hell to a heaven, compared to their lot
    Though humble and poor, whose lives incite
And train men's thinking that else were not.

XI.

What a test of all life
    Is the school-time strife!
Oh, who is he that shall win life's prize?—
He may be the least in his comrades' eyes.
For the compass that saves when mysteries
        throng
Would better be sensitive first than strong.
The triumph of sinew and speed are brief;

For the harbor sought is dim and far,
    Past many a bar,
And many a well hid reef.
From many a moon-lit bay men bless
    Bright beacons beck
    Toward death and wreck,
  And many are winds that rise and roar
    To drive ashore.
Ah me, the pilots of sure success
Sail not at random, nor steer by guess.
The voyage of life is a voyage for naught,
If souls keep not to one thing sought,
And never forget to give it their thought.

XII.

The new has claims
    That the old has not.
How much for games
    Is the home forgot!
There are sports for green and river and hall,
Kite and see-saw, fishing and ball,
Clubs and parties, music and fun,
Books to study and slight and shun,
And fresh little thoughts in tones that tinkle,
As dance the dimples that round them wrinkle,

More dear to refresh the soul with delight
Than all of their elders' reason and right.
For the healthful, heartful blush
    Of youth's fair spring-time's flower and fruit,
Is never the autumn's hectic flush
    Of a life that fades and dies at the root.

XIII.

Oh, where are the minds that pair
    With those that their own have outgrown,
Nor long for another to share
    In moods at one with their own?
How oft a prize may be won,
    How oft the applause of the throng,
Yet to him that hears the "Well done,"
    The whole world yet seems wrong!
He knows not why till a face
    With eyes that the soul shines through,
Forsakes all others, to trace
    And find his own that withdrew;
Till feelings as timid as his,
    Yet yearning for love, and alone,
Unveil all the mysteries
    That hide their soul from his own.
Oh, where is the peace on earth,
    In which more peace can blend,

Or pride in a loftier sense of worth,
　　Than follows the LOVE OF THE FRIEND?
Not all the doubts of the creeds
　　Can shake their faith who find
No selfishness back of the deeds
　　Of one pure sensitive mind.

> *They are not alone,*
> 　　*But a part of life's whole,*
> *Whom love, when shown,*
> 　　*Hath joined in soul.*

XIV.

The friends that in closeted hours confess
　　The faith so dear
　　　　That both possess,
　　When others are near,
　　Abide contented not to reveal,
　　But merely to feel,
　　　　In walking
　　　　Or talking,
　　　That some one is nigh
　　With a kindling eye;
And some one exults at their well earned pride.
To tattle of love were suicide.
　　No trumpet or drumming
　　Proclaims the coming

Of God on high to a spirit on earth.
Then wherefore of love, if it have any worth?

XV.

Dear vows, they are meant when made,
　Of friendship forever to last;
But there, where the morn's bright beams were
　　cast
　　On a world so fair
That all seemed like a dream of an Eden rare,
Can the rays of the sun as it sets bring shade.
　　But even the night
　　Holds the moon's mild light;
And whenever the sun return again,
　　The fields that flame
　　To its touch are the same;
And, whenever the loved return, ah, then,
　　For the soul there are joys,
　　Tho' the girls and the boys
Gaze out through the guises of women and men.

XVI.

How soon the tints of morn fade away,
And the sun is clouded, and skies are gray!
Whatever the promise of rest or of toil,
There never can be an earthly soil,

But flood and earthquake tear;
There never can be an earthly air,
But wind and lightning rend.
Vain then to think of an earthly friend
Whose love and help can last!
For all, whenever their day be past,
The air they breathe, the soil they tread
Will close in a coffin and leave them dead;
  And he that sought
  For the strength they brought

By himself alone
 Must make his quest
For a home to own
 In the land of the best.

XVII.

There comes a time that none can escape,
When each for himself a choice must make,
Must turn to a path that is right or is wrong,
And the path that he takes is a path life-long.
What though some weak, mild memory know
Not the hour nor the day that tested it so?
What though some shrink from the woes before
With a shock that is never forgotten more?—
All noted their paths, and thought of the change
Till nothing that came seem'd wholly strange;

And though there is little for curses or hymns
   In a thought of the earth or the skies,
Our wishes and ways are heirs of our whims,
   And our footsteps follow our eyes.
Great crimes can never their souls allure,
Who have kept their moods and memories pure,
        And so I know,
That the souls that hold to the right with ease,
  Have fought their vices before they fall.
      The time to stop sinning
      Is ere its beginning.
      Allow'd to grow,
The germs of guilt, like those of disease,
  Prove deadly because they seem so small.

XVIII.

How much we need this lesson, alas!
We sally forth: we mix with the mass:
We meet a world, too willing to show
How little about the world we know.
      When only a boy,
To know a little is all our joy.
      But alas, for a man,
His trials begin as Adam's began!
Like him, we all would be gods, and boast
Of knowledge and power to the uttermost.

16

When comes the day
Revealing how small
Is the sphere that life has allotted us all,
We choose a way
To rise or to fall;
We accept from above,
And use with love
Our partial dower,
And learn to master and make it a power;
Or we boast of what
Our souls have not,
And turn from the frank, fair ways of truth
To the ways that avoid it, and think, forsooth,
That nothing can shatter a sham defense
That hides our hollowness in pretense.

XIX.

Alas, if the world affect one so,
How suddenly old the young may grow!
No longer they seek for the right, too vain
To ask it, and make their ignorance plain.
No longer they struggle for love that lends
No more than frailty borrows from friends.
No longer they live in the light, but trust
Disguises that doom them to garbs of dust.

Oh earth, tho' royal the robes you bring,
They stifle the spirit to which they cling!
For none are free, when the truth shines bright,
Who would fly or hide themselves from sight.
   They are free alone,
Who dare to hold their souls to the light,
 And have their innermost motives known.

XX.

What joys are as great, since the world began,
 As the joy of the soul whose depths impart
  The LOVE OF THE LOVER that opens the
   heart
Of the man to the maid and the maid to the man!
The cup of life that was hollow and dry
   Is thrilling and filling
   And sparkling and spilling.
   Live high! is the cry;
Live high! as the glasses clash and jingle,
And currents of life in them mingle and tingle.
The spirit within has flooded each brim,
And eyes grow dizzy and dazed and dim.
Both drink till they reel, and around and around
The world goes whirling. Ah, never so bright
Was ever the world!—Their spirits have found

The realm of the stars, and at last caught sight
Past the sparks that are flying, the source of all
       light.

> *They are not alone,*
>   *But a part of life's whole*
> *Whom love, when shown,*
>   *Hath joined in soul.*

XXI.

There dawns, transfiguring earth and skies,
   A day in the light of which faith may be sure
   What power makes all life be and endure.
It comes, when, filling with hope, we rise
   Redeemed in soul by the Spirit of Truth;
And it comes with assent that glorifies
   A soul that has won the love of its youth.
      Ah, never the trills
Of the birds were half so thrillingly sweet;
      Nor ever the rills
Rolled on so clear at the feet.
      The leaves are all flowers,
      And crystal all showers.
Through the clouds the green hills loom, as grand
As the nearing shores of a spirit-land;

And the lights of the stars gleam down thro' a
    soul
That heaves like a wave of the infinite whole.
We float and fuse in the fragrant air;
We fade from ourselves; we die to all care.
Ay, she that is ours in that moment of bliss
Brings all immortality, worth not this.
Nay, nay, we have gain'd the life above.
Who dares to deny it to our first love?
We have, we have eternity!—Yet
The brightest of suns may rise to set.
How blest are they who never find out
How earthly love, like its home, shifts about!

XXII.

    Romance is a dream
      That the wise esteem,
For none whom it never possest
Were ever the bravest or best.
The helpers that bend to all need
Are sensitive first to heed
    The calls that are nearest.
The loving all learn the art
Of opening mind and heart
    With those that are dearest.

And, oh, wherever two souls agree
　　With every mood transparent within,
How pure they grow to the eyes that see,
　　How empty themselves of sin!

XXIII.

The spirit of love is far too rare
For ever deceit or doubt to dare,—
A hallow'd spirit whom awed delight
Must ever worship in robes of white.
Too oft by a touch that never was meant
The veil of its holy of holies is rent;
Too oft from a heedless impious tone
　　　　Love's glory has flown.
The souls that together lived in light,
They weep apart through the long, long night.

XXIV.

Where is hell?　Ah me, there is life on earth
Torn away from all it is worth.
Things are severed by nature allied:
Wish and all of its wants divide.
Who but the loving are dupes of hate?
Who but the faithful are foiled by fate?
Who but the seekers of truth can find
Half of the falsehood framed for the mind?

Who but those with ideals fair
Deal with a real life hard to bear?
True to an instinct cheating all trust,
Flapping white wings that raise but the dust,
Stuck like stones in the mire of the earth,
What for our souls are the bright stars worth!

XXV.

Love is the flame of a fire divine
Lit and fanned on an earthly shrine.
Heaven and earth both claim it their own.
Why should either let it alone?
Why should the earth not strive to show
That all of its traits belong below?
Why should the heaven be loathe to try
To prove that they all belong on high?
For the most of us men, betwixt the two,
The only things that are left to do
Are to grieve that the one has lowered our love,
Or to mourn that the other has borne it above.
Whichever life's plan,
It leaves the man

By himself alone
To make his quest
For a home to own
In the land of the best.

XXVI.

One seeks not to rhyme
An excuse for a crime,
Who speaks but a truth that is true in all time,
And says that the art
Of breaking the heart
Is not confined to one sex at the start.

Who are they that dance
With our early romance,
Alluring us on to love with a glance?
There are girls who decoy
The more modest boy,
Whose faith they entrap to treat like a toy.

Who are they that start
Their hand for our heart,
Then fling down the mitten to see how we smart?
They are maids who propose
That we love as do those
Who have flirted their limit of love to a close.

Who the most are adverse
To a man with no purse,
And smile if we think with no heart he is worse?

They are matrons who trade
The soul of the maid,
And the bride deem best who has been best paid.

Who are they that sigh
As we ask of them "Why?"
"There is nothing like learning.   You learn by
and-by"
They are women whose flings
At the sacredest things
Have poisoned all life in its life-giving springs.

XXVII.

Ah me, is it wisdom that makes men say
That feeling to frankness should never give way?
It surely is better to trust our own soul
And be true to ourselves than to others' control.
In love it is better to live while we live,
Than to wait till our ghost has nothing to give;
While all that is in us is yearning to band,
Give a heart for acceptance as well as a hand.
Love, rarest of passions, with burnings untold,
Refines all the being to turn out its gold.
One sound of their kindling, wrong hears as a
knell,
And sinks from that heaven as far as to hell.

He is curst who would clog with caution's alloy
What strengthens our virtue or sweetens our
    joy,
Who would chill into calmness what flows from
    the heart
Till it show but the ice-like sparkle of art.

XXVIII.

  Alas, the spirit, aspiring much,
    May find its vision flit at a touch!
What right has a mortal here to control
        Another in soul?—
  No more than a fiend, when starting to clutch,
      And drag another to dwell
        In its hell!—
      Yet oh, a fiend too
        Might deem it sweet
To know of a soul to his own soul true;
  And if their lips were to meet,
I think in the swoon that followed that kiss,
They might die to wrong, and awake in bliss.

XXIX.

How slightly the long years change our life!
We broke for a look and a whisper of strife;

We thought that the seasons the past would
    screen:
The winters were chill, but the spring was green.

We call'd up our passion and pride in their
    might;
But others we sought for, brought no delight.
We push'd through the city: we stroll'd through
    the park:
One spake in the silence; one moved in the dark.

We dream'd we could mould our being to stone:
Our heart became cold, and we wandered alone.
God made us for life; a statue we stood.
The surface felt smooth, and the world called us
    good.

But, anon, did the marble-like mien convulse,
The heart beat strongly, and warm flow the
    pulse,
The dull ear listen, the glaring eye see,
Oh love, that forgives, God's love is in thee!

XXX.

Behold, storm-toss'd in the night,
    The soul desponding hears,
Like the fiat of God at creation,
    The fiat of love, "Let there be light!"

And the air around one clears,
    And a radiant face appears,
Like a sun, and with it a revelation
    Of beauty and worth
    In heaven and earth.
Were they ever before so bright?
Was there ever such glory that burst from
    gloom
As the LOVE OF THE WEDDED PAIR, bride and
    groom?

> *They are not alone*
>   *But a part of life's whole,*
> *Whom love when shown,*
>   *Hath joined in soul.*

XXXI.

Now, over the will that slept
And dreamt of the guard it kept,
There steals the sweetest of powers to possess,
So like to the beauty of Holiness,
That ever, to souls that awake, it appeals
Like a vision that heaven itself reveals.
Is it something new or something old?
How can it be new and faith so bold?
How can it be old, and hope not cold?

Or can it be both?—so dull to the good,
Our souls wait long to learn what they should:
There is memory far more real than sight;
And a state immortal where age brings might.

XXXII.

An eye, when seeing
The sphere of being,
May look out through the senses, or else look in.
But looks each way, toward a different goal,
Toward hell through the senses and heaven
through the soul.
Who searches without and not within,
He thinks the good far off that is near;
And sees no heaven tho' heaven be here.
If that which he worship be worldly pelf,
Oh, he knows not
What souls have got
Whose God is the God of the inward self.
Oh, he knows not
Why such as they care never a jot,
That he finds fault
With the one that they so love and trust.
He may be just,
But judges by sight.
The things that are seen may all be white.
One's own is the sugar; the others' are salt.

XXXIII.

But who can trace
What is under a face?
Does a quiet mien
Tell of hope serene
From a spirit withdrawn, through inward grace,
To dwell in a realm where is no distress?
Or is it the stare
Of one dead to care,
Since dead to all but to selfishness?—
The brightest of glances,—oh trust it never!—
May flash from a passion to scorch forever.
Light brightens the sky
When a dawn is nigh,
Or when a volcano.—Some women, once wed,
Drop the smile from their face with the veil they
have shed.
Some men are suitors who offer their hands
Like the opening palms
Of beggars when kneeling and asking for alms;
But the one that pays heed
They clutch in their greed,
Turning fingers to fists and prayers to com-
mands.
What need of disguise when a prey is secure,
And divorce is disgrace in society pure?—

Soon, bird-like, flitting from homes unblest,
Their singing is all outside of their nest.

XXXIV.

What serpent is this
That would whisper and hiss
The damning advice
Of the first Paradise,—
That those who would equal the lords of creation
Must mount through force to a lordlier station?
True love forever fulfils the ideal
Of faith, that in loving, can love to kneel.
Ah me, what danger and doom may lurk,
Ye daughters of Eve, in a scheme that would
    wrest
From hearts that would give it,
Would ye but live it,
A sovereignty already possest!
Oh, how can a mortal dare to touch
And tarnish and bruise with an impious clutch
The finish of all creation's work,
Ere the hand of love
Was lifted above?
Oh, how can a spirit ever be proud
Of an ermine that fits it no more than a shroud?—

Of beauty that all is only a mask,
A label for death-drugs hid in a flask?—
Of sympathy waived for sharpness of eye?—
Of sweetness, for weakness that wins with a
    lie?

XXXV.

Far better than bodies that rot before
The breath has left them, and hold no more,
In the haunted hell that is glassed by their
    eyes,
A charm to inspire, a thought to make wise,—
Far better than these, the face as white
As ashes where dead fires drop their light;
Far better the eyes, all dim and dry,
But blind as one's own that can but cry;
Far better the crape and the veils that fall;
Far better the living room turned to a pall.
All these, whatever the future may give,
Have proved that love has a right to live,

Though all alone
*   One make his quest*
For a home to own
*   In the land of the best.*

XXXVI.

Oh why do we sever, and bound to the fray,
And spurn contentment and court dismay!
We buckle in pleasure; we buckle on pain;
We tighten the sinews that tingle and strain;
We wrench at the nerve's frail fibers until
We have snapped the tenderest cord with our
    skill,
Till no matter what may touch the strings
No note of harmony longer rings.
We are off in the dark, down, down for boons
Where never come suns, where never come
    moons.
Nay, that is not half of the woe, not half;
We lie to our nature; we twit and we laugh;
       We dare
To jeer of a love that was ours,
       We dare, yet there
Through thorns and tares are living the flowers!

XXXVII.

Unhelpt by any, what power can save
The lonely spirit that earth would enslave?
    Aface that test
That ever awaits to waylay the best,
Shall one, when the world

17

Asserts control,
Forget the soul?
With every flag of a high cause furl'd
Give up his fight for virtue and truth,
And become a man of the world, forsooth?—
Ay, ay, a coward, who cringed and bow'd,
And has grown content to court the crowd?—
A mountebank who, in storm or calm,
Turns up or down his willing palm
For a pittance from snobs that he thinks to
    please
With a sneer for those and a smile for these?

XXXVIII.

Full many are paths where life can guide us.
Whichever we take from some they divide us.
Wherever we go, and follow men not,
No slight of their leading is ever forgot;
    The best of our deeds is quoted as bad;
Once John had a devil; once Christ was a sot.
    Our toil—what of it?—is lonely and sad.
But God made us all, in spite of the throng
Who deem us, if not like themselves, made wrong.
God rules: then perchance we are wiser for deeds
That learn from feelings as much as from creeds,

When taught thro' the injuring zeal of our race
That gentleness shows a growth in grace;
When taught with Him, whose patience mild
Sigh'd only to point the man to the child.

XXXIX.

When the world began,
What gave it light
Was the touch of love's electric might.
That touch still brings, in the heavenly plan,
The spark of the spirit that makes man man.
His life all starts in a flash of light,
A gleam of glory, blessed and bright,
The while within him is lighted a fire
Where burns forever the soul's desire;
And all he owns that gives him worth
Is that inward glow that shines for earth,
And shows the love that gave it birth.

XL.

Let husband and wife
Be parted in strife;
Or indifference worse, like a wedge, be driven
Dividing the two whose vows were given
The one to the other;

Still, still, how oft, as the years go by,
A feeble voice and a helpless cry
May, far from the depths of the soul, conjure
The LOVE OF THE PARENT, and sweetly assure
    The father and mother

> *That none are alone*
>   *But a part of life's whole,*
> *Whom love, when shown,*
>   *Hath joined in soul.*

XLI.

The touch of the tenderest hands,
   Where lives were rent in twain,
May weld again with the sturdiest bands
   The broken links of love's dear chain.
All filled with a father's pride,
The groom again has a bride,
And thrilled by the hope in store
The bride has a groom once more.

XLII.

Behold in the parent the world's first priest,
To tender, till childhood's wants have ceast,

The flickering fires
That fall and rise in rash desires;
To soothe and assuage,
In a body that thirsts and soul that aspires,
The wishes of youth with the wisdom of age;
To kneel or to stand
With a mission more grand
Than any but His whose touch divine
First lit the flame on the human shrine,
Then left it alone where all men try
To fan its burning or find it die.

XLIII.

And what are the laws for word or deed
Of the priest whose ministry all will heed?
Oh, what but laws of that in the soul
Which starts the life that the laws control?
Ah me, if to love we owe life's giving,
It must be love that rules right living!
If thought be that which has gone astray,
Then love must lead to the wiser way.
No fighting of error by force does aught
But change the statement not the thought.
To ponder and halt
Are seldom all fault;

A natural smile
　　Has in it no guile;
But many a false array of zeal
Has frightened from frankness, and so from
　　weal;
And many a blast of pious hate
Been blown by the devil to train his mate.

XLIV.

If deeds go astray, no force men know
Can check what nature has made to flow.
If wrong attract, and right estrange,
Then love must enter, and subtly change
What courses forth from the soul below.
Oh, nothing of good can life secure
Save when the springs of life are pure!
　　When this they be,
　　　　Their earliest vent,
　　As mad and free
As a mount's cascade, may all seem spent
　　In dashing away
　　To spatter and spray,
　　But yet may go
　　In an onward flow
To flood wide valleys where buds are elate,
And fruit is forming, and harvests wait.

XLV.

How early, alas, do the sheltering walls
Of the home reecho the world's loud calls!
   No more, at the start,
Than the note of a playfellow's drum or fife,
  Anon, from field, or haven, or mart,
     Is heard
     A word
From messmate, partner, sweetheart, wife,
And the ward that was has left for life.

XLVI.

'T is well when two who love must sever
If neither be taken from earth forever.
'T is well for those of a ward bereft
If hope of helping him still be left.
How sad when the one we had led by the hand
Who had looked to us for every demand
Of body or soul has gone to the grave,
And we must live, not die as we crave,
But watch him pass to the sunless gloom
Beyond that mile-stone mark of the tomb,
And, led by those whom never he knew,
Go journeying on the darkness through,

As all alone
  He makes his quest
For a home to own
  In the land of the best!

XLVII.

When children have grown and bear no trace
Of that which charmed in the childhood-face,
How well for the parent whose love but sought
For the growth of their spirits in love and
    thought!
          How blest is their lot
          Whose parting means not
A parting of soul!   How blest is the mother
          Whose boy is her lover!
How blest is the father who seems but a brother!
How blest all the household who all discover
That even a babe's life just begun
Has a heart and a head that must be won;
That the youngest will with a wish has rights
    For all to respect!
Ah, what is there human that nature slights,
  And what in life that love can neglect!
The petty desire of the tenderest tone
To God is as great and as dear as one's own.

XLVIII.

Oh, would that to love one's child and kind
And, no matter how men differ in mind,
To give to each a right to bear
      His own soul where
The spirit within him and world outside
And God in both essay to guide,—
Oh, would that these could insure for each
That soul-communion that all would reach!
But no; whoever would seek high aims
Must oft forego all lower claims.
      Not a few there are
      Move on so far
      That never a man
      Helps on their plan,
      Nor a confidant's voice
      Confirms their choice.
There are years for them, when the loveliest face
Seems only a framing wherein to trace
A part of an interest felt in the race.
      But oh,
    Let us believe they grow,
The farther that thus they leave behind
The common paths of all mankind,
The higher the sound of their spirit's call,
If the less to one, the more to all.

XLIX.

No search for the truth with a willing mind
Is a search for what one is willing to find,
But a search for the willing of all mankind.
Who seek but this, though many may leave them
And loss of all in the home may grieve them,
At last may slowly learn to trace
Fair traits of the spirit in each new face;
And with LOVE OF THE FELLOWMAN, turning
    from none,
Come, at last, to find earth's family one.
In the current of life, wherever it rolls,
Like drops in the sea are our separate souls;
And the wind and the wave of the stormy weather
That dash them apart may dash them together,

> *For none are alone*
> *But a part of life's whole,*
> *Whom love, when shown,*
> *Hath joined in soul.*

L.

Oh, why should a mortal from mortal part!
No beauty was ever revealed in art
Where rhythm and tone or color and line
        Did not combine;

And beauty of life was never one's own
Who, when he had sought it, sought it alone.

LI.

The world is a ship that sails through space;
   And men are voyagers journeying where
One destiny waits for all the race,
   One common port for joy or care.
Why not, like travelers, launched at sea,
   Join hands and hearts, and, in every way,
If heaven be love, wherever we be,
   Begin the heaven we seek to-day?

LII.

Alas for the will of which men boast,
We all may lose what blesses us most!
      No wonder of old
      The world was told
That the first of our race with thought or voice
Broke loose from the cords that bound his choice,
His earliest cry: "The brave have deserts.
      Let the tree be our quest.
      In its fruit is food
      That is more than a test.
      The will that asserts

Its right to command,
And calls up the good
And the evil, shall stand
The equal of God—for whose wrath who cares?
All hail to a heaven for him who dares!"
Alas for the finite with strength so slight!
The equal of God must have infinite might.

LIII.

Some more, some less, with little to love,
We all to the sky oft leave the dove.
We delve away in the depth of our trade;
And all get dusty before well paid.
Some like the dust; some mourn its need;
And some are only intent to succeed.
Too may grow prostitutes, hugging to all,
Good, bad, or indifferent, beauty or scall,
Till all wishes that worth would have kept
Die out of the man unwept.
No pride or shame for himself or his kind
Brings up to the cheek one blush.
Whatever is there is a counterfeit flush,—
Mere paint on the surface of sham behind.

LIV.

There are times when the vilest of men disguises
His foulness in forms that love most prizes;

But alas! his gracious and graceful gait
The vilest of men takes on too late.
It never appears like a natural trait.
Nor long, I deem, will his mien cajole
      Those finding the whole
Of the sweet in his coating and not in the
    soul.
Who tastes that dainty, alas, but gnashes
At apples of Sodom!—he bites into ashes.
As well pursue a will-o'wisp's flare!—
His fire of devotion is all in the air.
As well touch a carcass!—those pulsings avow'd
Are worms that go crawling round under a
    shroud.
No soul is within him our soul to accost.
His might, not right, of repentance is lost.
The glut of the senses, like vultures above
A life that is dead, leaves nothing to love.

LV.

Sad, sad, indeed, is the lot of those
Whom no one mourns when their coffins close.
How lone, when the robes of earth-life fall,
Are spirits that hear no welcoming call;
Are spirits that see no smile of delight,
But, flying in shame from all things bright,

And, hiding in horror themselves have made,
Live ever in sunshine and know but shade,

As all alone
  They make their quest
For a home to own
  In the land of the best !

LVI.

  But even with sin
  May rescue begin,
  And out of a fall
  Come the safety of all,—
Come the knowledge of good and as well as of
    bad,
With the knowledge of ill from the shade of the
    sad,
The knowledge of faith which alone can unite
A soul to the Infinite source of light.

LVII.

It must have been in the years gone long
When the world was young, and men went
    wrong,
That love it was parted them all, and was able
To hinder earth's ill by a flood or a Babel,—

To make life's disciplined right succeed
Through the law of the Persian and lance of
    the Mede;
And where truth moved on, tho' few might know
    it,
To rule by the meek and to lead by the poet

LVIII.

If ever the mind to faith be brought,
Is it love that shall rule the inward thought?
Is it love that shall rule the outward life
And crown both source and sum of strife?—
Is it only that which springs from the heart
      That can ever impart
What fills the veins with vigor infused
And thrills the limbs with strength to be used?
Is it only this that can ever fulfill
The way of the world's Creator's will,
      And thus create
      That heavenly state
For which men work the while they wait?

LIX.

What bliss, when gazing, dazed and dim,
Down through the depths of mystery
From which creation's wonders brim,
To dream that all evolves above

A source that is ever the LOVE OF LOVE!—
Whose rule is a rule of sympathy,
Whose law is a law of liberty,
 Whose home of union
 A holy communion

   Where none are alone
    But a part of life's whole,
   Whom love, when shown,
    Hath joined in soul!

LX.

Life is a mystery, mystery-bound.
Above or about us no rest is found;
But, center'd in every cycling change,
If one hope draw us, wherever we range,
Then must it be that the soul inclined
To merely an earthly love must find
  With each new light
  That cheers the sight
The shaft of a corridor stretched afar
To where the glories of all love are,—
A shaft to whiten and brighten the way
To a hall and home where ends the day,
And heaven and earth, life's groom and bride,
Shall gather their children, trained and tried,

And those that have learned
What faith has earned,
Shall sleep the slumber of all the blest
And dream the dreams of an endless rest.

SONNETS.

THE LEADER.

THE wind swept toward him, and the sunlight
    glanced
From his bright armor, but the smoke and dust
Hid all his comrades in a train august
Trailed from him, as in splendor he advanced.
We deemed him leader, yet he merely chanced
To be where all things round him could adjust
To his position wind and sun, and thrust
On him a prominence naught else enhanced.
Oh blame not wind or sun, nor envy him!
What though the world too highly rate his worth?
Who, who, for this, would choose a rôle so mean,
So distant from the clouds that always dim
The central fight?—It is one law of earth
That godlike leaders work, like God, unseen.

———

THE SOLITARY SINGER.

WHIRRED like the moulting wings of some
    vast swan,
The snow-blast broods above the landscape
    drear;

But through the wild wind shivers, high and
    clear,
The call of one lone bird that sings anon.
Sing on, thou child of warmth and light, sing on!
I know thy loneliness, I know thy cheer.
Thy call will never bring one comrade near,
Nor make the world about less chill and wan.
But, oh, no tempest can outblow, sweet bird,
Those drafts thine ardent spirit draws to bring
The breath of heaven to fill thy trembling breast,
So thrilled to voice the world's Creator's word!
Whom God inspires, though they unheeded sing,
May be through mere expression wholly blest.

STAKING ALL.

BETTER to stake one's all on some high cause
    And lose, than never know the spirit's thrill
When gates of heaven are seen, past mortal ill,
Though light that bursts from them at once
    withdraws.
'T is not the accent of this world's applause
That marks the rhythm of the songs that fill
Heaven's vault, and, with their sweetness, well-
    nigh still
The wings of angels, tempted then to pause.

Things viewed or heard can bring us bliss alone
When, moved to pass beyond each earthly wall,
And borne to hights mere feet have never trod,
We reach a region far above our own,
Where all souls live for one and one for all,
And each finds full companionship with God.

OBSCURITY.

DEEM not thyself a slave because assigned
    To small obscurity where few can view
Thy steadfast industry, thy purpose true,
Thy sacrifice that seems all undivined.
The feet that tread the treadmill no more bind
The spirit to their petty task, than do
Our brains bind thought whose words, by
    working through,
Not in, this mortal framework, lead their kind.
Full many a blaze-mailed knight men's cheers
    allure
To wrong by which mere groundling-praise is
    won;
While serfs, though soil-stained, keep life's re-
    cord pure
Because their dust-hid deeds are wrought for
    none

Save One for whom no life is too obscure
To show the spirit in which work is done.

INFLUENCE.

OH, for the hope that once inspired my tongue
　　Ere life had known of all these weary
　　　　years,—
Sad nights whose dreams were launched in
　　silent tears,
And sadder days whose deeds to wreck were
　　flung!
How nobler had my purpose died when young,
Not numbed by blows, and not abashed by
　　jeers,
Nor hounded by a world of clubs and spears
To make faith fly to cover, cowed and stung!
Yet why judge influence by what most men
　　prize?
Must that which leads the spirit have recourse
To what attracts to station, or to guise?
Naught draws life heavenward like the sun-
　　light's force.
But sunlight never blest one man with eyes
Lured but to gaze upon its blinding source.

THE FINAL VERDICT.

ACCEPT men's judgment of my work?—
　　Not one
Knows what I do, or why.　I will not heed
Those guessing how my structure may succeed
From scaffoldings about it, scarce begun.
I will not think with those who would let none
But some "old master" dictate my new deed,
As if a plan to fit the future's need
Could all be fashioned on what once was done!
Deem not the worthiest art-work wrought by
　　those
Whose thoughts and aims are easiest to find.
Full oft the purpose that it subtly shows
Will long elude the keenest searching mind;
And, sometimes, not before this life shall close
Can what it means for spirit be divined.

THE CHANCE THAT COMES TO
EVERY MAN

THE chance that comes to every man—the
　　chance!
Ah, but it does not come to every man.
The hero finds a place not in his plan,
And, while he fills it well, the lines advance,

The bugle calls, the flashing weapons glance;
The smoke of conflict hides the shouting van,
And glory comes; but he, as he began,
He guards the rear,—a slave of circumstance.
The greatest victory may be quickest won;
And they who happen to be in the lead
Are hailed as leaders, and the rest as led.
But, oh, the work, ere fighting had begun!
The drill! the foresight!—Well, some men suc-
ceed,
And some do not, and soon will all be dead.

HEREDITY.

WE know not whence came manhood; but
we know
Whence came the man,—from unfulfilled de-
sire
When springs that welled from body quenched
the fire
That burned to fuse in one two souls aglow.
Embodiment of wish, on earth below,
For union which no earth-forms can acquire,
Man is a spirit, aimed for regions higher,
Entrapped and èntrailed in a world of woe.

What wonder if he wander on and on
Through ways that bring no respite and no rest?
What wonder if no crown that shines upon
His brow can ever sate ambition's quest?
What wonder if death only end, anon,
A strife that never one deems wholly blest?

UNCONSCIOUS CHARM.

UNCONSCIOUS of their charm, the wind-
swayed trees
Their welcomes wave; and hills with flower-lined
ways
Rise dawn-like, and, bedimmed with morning
haze
Like incense visible, make sweet the breeze.
And, all unconscious of their charm as these,
The fair, sweet children pass me in their plays,
Nor dream that seeing them one joy conveys
To me whom they feel no desire to please.
Ah, thus unconscious, must each human will
Inspire enchantment in a fellow-soul?
Vain then to hope that our mere toil or skill
Can gain our life or art its lordliest rôle.
The spirit's touch that stirs the spirit's thrill
Starts in a source too deep for man's control.

IN THE ART-MUSEUM.

FAR in the dome the limnered angels poise
    Above high cliffs of columns; while, below,
The tiles gleam like a sunset-lake aglow
When with each wavelet some new sunbeam toys.
Now from without a troop of loud-heeled boys
And shrill-voiced girls come bounding, then,
    more slow,
Proceed on tiptoe, whispering as they go,
Their whole demean the ghost of former noise.
No temple this, yet sacred none the less
Through art, the handcraft that transcribes
    man's best
In feeling, thought, and skill, the wage of duty.
Ah, well man's best may make this earth seem
    blest!
The dim-veiled beauty of God's holiness
Looms always through art's holiness of beauty.

THE CLIMBER.

FROM youth these mounts have lured me on,
    until
In age I stand amid their frost and snow;
And but when searching back through vales
    below

Descry what once inspired my tireless will.
First, youth's hot fever, then numb age's chill,
And naught between them of enjoyment, oh,
Why could my life's long effort never know
Rewards that could repay my toil and skill?
Can it be true that aims too grand, too high,
May miss the garden sought, where, hour by
    hour,
The fellow-workers in new Edens meet?
Can but the small seed's growing, by-and-by,
Engarland all one's paths with leaf and flower,
And keep the world he lives in fresh and sweet?

SENSE AND SOUL.

L ET not mere earthly forms, however bright,
    Keep us of heaven's high glory unaware.
They are but vehicles of life they bear
Up toward the portals of eternal light.
Let no one take the lamps men hang at night
For stars that never leave the upper air;
Or think a dawn worth while comes anywhere
Except where skies and sunlight bring the sight.
Shame on the groundling thought that always
    weighs
Against endangered rights that call aloft

Its own low interests it would guard too well.
What though these fall like cinders from the
　　blaze
Of love too ardent?　Ours are souls that oft
We strip for heaven by flinging sense to hell.

————

CLASS AND CASTE.

CLASS me not with your classes,—me who
　　came
From God, and common dust!　I will not don
These robes, these badges, nay, nor be whirled
　　on
Behind the liveries that high state proclaim.
For me no earthly splendor shall outflame
Heaven's light, or that high realm it shines upon;
No earthly station satisfy, anon,
Aims that arrested there would rest in shame.
For him who judges manhood by its best
There is no noblest rank not won by soul,
No throne worth seeking reached on steps of
　　sod,
No life that ever can seem wholly blest
But feels itself a part of that great whole,
At one with which is being one with God.

THE FAITH THAT DOUBTS.

THE church-bell tolls; the organ tones begin;
    Bright liveries flaunt the advent of the
        proud;
And, thronged through aisles in silks that rustle
        loud,
The world without becomes the church within.
With incantations exorcising sin,
The white-robed choir and priests have marched
        and bowed;
And pleas, politely phrased to please the crowd,
Have flattered those whose coin the coffers win.
And thus, forsooth, with lip and eye and ear
Men seek to honor him whose one chief call
Was "Follow me." Were they to meet him here,
Could those whose faith these outward forms
        enthrall
Trust to the spirit in him, or revere
The kind of living for which he gave all?

BROADENING ONE'S OUTLOOK.

OH, not the outward things that may incite
    Give the true measure of the inward aim!
Our minds are deeper than our deeds proclaim;
And only thought can make them move aright.

In youth all secret loathings leap to light.
We hunt for what has caused them as for game,
Blow loud our horns, and him they halt not
　　　blame;
Nor rest till nothing hostile loom in sight.
In age, grown mild, we rather would not see
The forms once fought, we rather would not
　　　mind
Than mend the lack of traits once highly prized.
Ah, has the earnest aim then ceased to be?
Or have our thought-trained spirits learned to
　　　find
Some worth in things that once we but despised?

OUR AFFINITY.

IN that dear sport where Cupid leads the chase,
　　Of heavenly light is framed each gentle dart;
And where it speeds, with photographic art,
It leaves an image nothing can efface.
No laws for merely seed and soil debase
The methods used for love within the heart.
That heart responds, before a sprout can start,
With flower and fruit whose growth no seasons
　　　trace.

Yes, all through life, whenever come in view
Those helping spirits, always on the quest
For moods too like their own moods to rebuff
The thought that is to their own thinking true,
To know our own twin angel from the rest,
One touch, one look, one accent is enough.

MY ACTRESS.

HER pictures, not herself, affect me so, —
Her finished photographs, but not the
plates
Where alchemy's dark conjuring creates
What rises from the glassy deeps below.
My life is loveless, and her play can show
That which I might have loved, and so it mates
And cheers my soul, the while lone wish awaits
The spirit-form that haunts the life I know.
Real lovers, hand in hand, may fail to see
How she, with feigned familiarities,
Can make more firm my faith in my ideal.
Ah, they wot not that life has left to me
But dreams of that which might be, not what is;
And, while no dream holds her, I feel them
real.

19

THE FIRST FASCINATION.

ACROSS the threshold of this life below,
　　Oft comes a form more sacred than of
　　　　friend,
With which, entranced by love, we onward wend,
Our thoughts, our cheeks, our pulses all aglow.
Oh, ye that boast uprightness, do ye know
How sweet a tone might then have bid it end?
Were such not heard or heeded, 't will be
　　kenned
Some day that some good angel made it so.
Thou first of lovers, when this life goes by,
Its lists made out and all things understood,
If right be ours, what shall we owe the touch
Of thy dear hand, and thy pure word and eye!
The saved think less that they themselves were
　　good
Than that they were not tempted overmuch.

THE LOST FRIEND.

I WOULD not doubt your word,—nor could
　　gainsay
The proof you show me, blind be to that fire
Which, blazing in the torch of your desire,
Makes all my night of doubt as bright as day.

But side by side with him through all the way
I toiled till now; nor ever could aspire
To aught past where he seemed to call me higher,
And lead straight onward, if I dared to stray.
Why, we were like two arms that limb one frame,
Two hands that ply one work, two eyes that trace
One onward path, two ears that heed the same
Inciting cry, two steeds that lead the race
Yoked to one car, twin rivals for one aim, —
To think my friend base, I myself were base.

FOR A BOOK MADE UP OF CONTRIBU-
TIONS FROM AUTHORS.

OH, not for wealth or fame do poets yearn
  With ardor fired to burnish phrase and
    line!
Nay, not for this! Their fervor would enshrine
In forms as bright bright thoughts that in them
  burn.
What luck is mine, then, freed from all concern
About how I a setting may design
To make my paste another's gem outshine?
My light, though slight, a beacon's place may
  earn!

Less due to oil than to reflectors round
A wick's weak flicker is the blaze that blinds.
How mine should blaze for you, then, gazing at
This offering, haloed all about, ray-bound
By bright reflections of the brightest minds!—
Art's proof is in the setting.   Judge by that.

FORD'S GLEN,

WILLIAMSTOWN.

WHEN first I followed up thy modest brook,
And left the northwest road, and came
on thee,
How grand thy wood-crowned rocks appeared
to be
Whose high-arched foliage heaven's dim light
forsook!
But when, years later, I came back to look
On what so awed, I stood amazed to see
How small and shrunk, when shorn of every
tree,
Were all that I for lofty cliffs mistook.
Then, in my college-town, I joined, once more,
The mates I so had honored in my youth.

Alas, in some, no mystery seemed to lurk
Where hights of promise had so loomed of yore!
Has life no sphere in which one finds, forsooth,
No wrong to nature wrought by man's mean
    work?

PRINCETON UNIVERSITY.

WELL placed, my Princeton, on the fore-
    most range
Where Allegheny uplands first appear
Bent down to greet the sea, bent up to rear
What walls our continent of rock and grange!
If English sires, too loyal to seek change,
Their Kingston, Queenston, Princeton founded
    here,
It made no Witherspoon nor Stockton fear
A throne that dared their new land's rights
    estrange.
Nor now shall Princeton, welcoming to her
    school
The thought of Europe, find her own less bold
Because of that which from abroad is drafted.
Let stay thy "classics"! No one not a fool
To get new learning need forget the old;
And minds, like fruit-trees, bear their best when
    grafted.

IN PRINCETON CEMETERY.

THERE are few kindred places on the earth
 Where rest as many great men as lie here;
Or, in proportion, more men to revere
Of those whose learning was outweighed by
 worth.
Not strange then that, at many a household-
 hearth
And student desk, our generation fear
To change or question aught these men held dear;
As if, forsooth, a saint could need new birth!
Yet all whose learning brings them fame to last
Begin by doubting what earth claims it knows.
Why should not their true follower do the same?
Think not the present can but phase the past.
The fire whose dying brand so steadfast glows
Once proved its life through flickerings of its
 flame.

IN BONAVENTURE CEMETERY,

SAVANNAH.

THE live-oak's bending boughs, gray-draped
 in moss,
Like mourning sentinels, guard the winding
 ways;

But under them each grave the eye surveys
Is wreathed with flowers that breezes gently
    toss.
Ah, if the bowed oaks fitly frame our loss,
Beneath them crowd, too, symbols of the bays
To crown our loved ones in those far, fair days
That nights end not and storms can never
    cross.
Though bodies fail, souls need not meet de-
    feat.
Nay, let our spirits rise above like these
Blithe birds that, winged from out sweet flowery
    beds,
Soar up and sing through clouds of moss-hung
    trees,
Sing as of dreams of beauty, sure to greet
The slumber on which God such beauty spreads.

THE GRAVE OF GENIUS.

TREAD softly. Nothing mortal we revere
    Within the dwelling that we stand before.
No form will come to meet us from the door.
Only the spirit of the man is near.
Only to spirit do men ever rear

These shafts like arms uplifted to implore
The world to honor those we see no more,
But whose white souls the white tomb symbols
    here.
Ah, what could ever lead earth's dull throngs on
To those bright goals, concealed from mortal
    view
In future glory for which good men plan,
Except some spirit heaven had shone upon?
Our awe for genius is a worship due
To that which comes from God and not from
    man.

SONGS AND HYMNS.

FROM VARIOUS SOURCES PUBLISHED AND NOT PUBLISHED.

WHERE DWELL THE GODS?

WHERE dwell the gods?
　　Where dwell the gods?
Oh, dwell they in the sky?
Or come they near in gloom or gleam
Of earth or air or wood or stream?
　Oh, yes, the gods are all on high;
But, robed in all that teem or seem
　Where eye can spy or fancy fly,
　　The gods are always nigh.

　　How speak the gods?
　　How speak the gods?
　In thunder from the sky?
In storms that o'er the cloud-banks pour,
Or dash in waves along the shore?
　Oh, yes, the gods are all on high;
But not alone in rush and roar,
　Wherever breeze or breath can sigh
　　The gods are always nigh.

How touch the gods?
How touch the gods?
Oh, reach they from the sky
Wherever airy fingers brush
The leaves that throb, the cheeks that flush?
Oh, yes, the gods are all on high;
But in the thrills that fill the hush
When naught without is passing by,
The gods are always nigh.

Where look the gods?
Where look the gods?
In glances from the sky?
Down through the lightning's death-dealt blaze,
Or thrilling through the starry rays?
Oh, yes, the gods are all on high;
But in the looks that on us gaze
From out the love-lit human eye
The gods are always nigh.

—Written for "The Aztec God."

ALL HAIL THE GOD!

ALL hail the god!   All hail and laud
The god we now enthrone,
Whose realms extend, all bright and broad,
Beyond the seas and stars and aught

That ears have heard, or eyes have sought,
    Or hands could ever own.
All hail the god!   All hail the god!
    Upon the man we call;
But bright behind the gaze we greet,
There gleams a glory yet to meet
Our souls beholding past the gloom
Of toil and trouble, tear and tomb,
    The god beyond it all.

All hail the god!   All hail and laud
    The god we bow before,
Whose altar fires, while all are awed,
Are lit in souls that flash through eyes
That light for heaven itself supplies,
    Nor could one wish for more.
All hail the god!   All hail the god!
    Upon the man we call;
But bright behind the gaze we greet,
There gleams a glory yet to meet
Our souls beholding past the gloom
Of toil and trouble, tear and tomb,
    The god beyond it all.

—Idem.

OH, NOT WHAT LIFE APPEARS TO BE.

OH, not what life appears to be,
　　Is what in life is true.
Inveiled behind the forms we see
　　Are things we cannot view.
What but the spirit working through
The guise men wear to what they do
Reveals the force that, foul or fair,
Awakes and makes the nature there?

The sunshine shows the worth of suns,
　　The moisture, of the shower;
The stream of rills from which it runs,
　　The fragrance, of the flower;
And, oh, the spirit when it springs
Above the reach of earthly things,
As fall the limbs that feed the shrine,
Reveals the life to be divine.
　　　　　—Written for "The Aztec God."

ALL HAIL THE SUN.

ALL hail the sun that brings the light,
　　All hail the rays that shower,
And wake the barren wastes of night
　　To germ and leaf and flower.

All hail the life behind the sun,
    All hail the gods that dwell
Where men whose earthly race is run
    Are borne, and all is well.

All hail the form of him who dies,
    All hail the soul that wends
Up through the skies, and onward hies.
    All hail the gods, our friends.
                  —*Idem.*

O LIFE DIVINE.

O LIFE divine, from thee there springs
    All good that germs and grows,
Thy Light behind the sunlight brings
    The harvests to their close.

O Life divine, thou art the source
    Of truth within the soul;
Thou art the guide through all the course
    That leads it to its goal.

O Life divine, what soul succeeds
    In aught on earth but he
Who moves as all desires and deeds
    Are lured and led by thee!
            —*Written for "Columbus."*

O GOD OF ALL THINGS LIVING.

O GOD of all things living,
　　Our Sovereign, Saviour, Guide,
All gifts are of Thy giving,
　　All gains by Thee supplied.
　　　　The stars that make
　　　　High aims awake
Are but what Thine eye seest.
　　　　The stroke and stress
　　　　That earn success
Are but what Thou decreest.
O God of all things living,
　　Our Sovereign, Saviour, Guide,
All gifts are of Thy giving,
　　All gains by Thee supplied.

O God, all good bestowing
　　On souls that seek Thy way,
Our hearts, with joy o'erflowing,
　　Give thanks to Thee to-day.
　　　　In all the past
　　　　Whose blessings last,
Thy presence fills the story;
　　　　And all the gleams
　　　　That gild our dreams
Obtain from Thee their glory.

O God, all good bestowing
On souls that seek Thy way,
Our hearts, with joy o'erflowing,
Give thanks to Thee to-day.
—*Written for "Columbus."*

HAIL TO THE HERO, HOME FROM STRIFE.

HAIL to the hero, home from strife,
Pride of our hearts and hope of our life,
Hail to his glancing crest and plume,
Flashed like lightning into the gloom.
Hail to the grit that, when borne from view,
Out of the darkness brought him through,
Sprout of the slough-pit, bud of the thorn,
After the night
The light of the morn.
Crown him with flowers and cull them bright.
Crown him, the man of the land's delight.

Hail to the hero, home from strife,
Pride of our hearts and hope of our life.
Hail to the ring of the voice that taught
Drumming and roaring the rhythm of thought.

20

Hail to the tone that could change to a cheer
Groan and shriek of a startled fear,
Hushing to rills the flood that whirred,
     Chorusing night
     With songs of the bird.
Shout him a welcome, and shout with might,
Shout for the man of the land's delight.

          —*Written for "Columbus."*

O SOUL, WHAT EARTHLY CROWN.

O SOUL, what earthly crown
    Is bright as his renown
     Whose tireless race
Outruns the world's too halting pace,
To reach, beyond the things men heed,
That which they know not of, but need!

    O soul, what man can be
    As near to Christ as he
     Who looks to life
Not first for fame and last for strife;
But shuns no loss nor pain that brings
The world to new and better things!

          —*Idem.*

ALL HAIL THE QUEEN!

ALL hail the Queen!
    No thrills can fill the lover's breast
For that first love he loves the best,
Like ours that throb to each appeal
   Of her in whom, enthroned above
The nation's heart, we see, we feel
   The symbol of the sway we love,
   The while we hail our Queen.

All hail the Queen!
No cause can rouse the soul of strife
In men who war for child and wife,
Like ours that, where her battles be,
   Know not of rest until, above
The foe that falls, enthroned we see
   The symbol of the sway we love,
   The while we hail our Queen.

All hail the Queen!
No loyalty can make a son
Show what a mother's love has done,
Like ours who press through land and sea,
   Our one reward to find above
Our gains that show what man can be,
   The symbol of the sway we love,
   The while we hail our Queen.   —*Idem.*

WE LIVE BUT FOR BUBBLES.

WE live but for bubbles, and those who
    know
The way of the world their bubbles will blow.
Ay, all but whose doings are fated to be
No more than are drops in an infinite sea,
Will blow them, and show them, till, by and by,
They fill and float to the air on high;
Hoho! hoho! and the world will thus
Know how big a bubble can come from us.

We live but for bubbles that grow and glow
The bigger and brighter the more we blow;
And, borne on the breath of the breeze around
Wherever the tides of the time are bound,
There is nothing of earth or of heaven in sight
But they image it all in a rainbow light;
Hoho! hoho! and the world will thus
Know how bright a bubble can come from us.

We live but for bubbles a-dance in the blast,
But who can tell how long they will last?
So swell your cheeks, and puff, and fan,
And make the most of them while you can,
For if ever the breath in them fail, they will pop,
And only be drizzles to dry as they drop;

Hoho! hoho! and the world will thus
Be done with the bubbles that come from us.
  —*Written for "Cecil the Seer."*

OH, WHO HAS KNOWN.

OH, who has known the whole of light,
    That knows it day by day,
Where suns that make the morning bright,
    At evening, pass away?
Before the day, beyond the day,
    Above the suns that roll,
There was a light, there waits **a light**
    That never leaves the soul.

Oh, who has weighed the worth of **light**
    That gauged it by the gleam
That came within the range of **sight**,
    And thought the rest a dream?
Before that sight, beyond that sight
    And all that mortals deem,
There was a light, there waits a light,
    Where things are all they seem.
                          —*Idem.*

TWO SPRINGS OF LIFE.

TWO springs of life,—in air and earth;
    Two tides,—in soul and sod;
Two natures,—wrought of breath and birth;
    Two aims,—in cloud and clod;—
Oh, where were worlds, or where were worth
    Without the two, and God?

Two movements in the heaving breast;
    Two, in the beating heart;
Two, in the swaying soldier's crest;
    Two, in the strokes of art;—
Oh where in aught of mortal quest,
    Are e'er the two apart?

Two times of day,—in gloom and glow;
    Two realms—of dream and deed;
Two seasons—bringing sod and snow;
    Two states—of fleshed and freed;—
Oh where is it that life would go,
    But through the two they lead?

Two frames that meet,—the strong, the fair,
    True love in both begun;
Two souls that form a single pair;
    Two courses both have run;—

Oh where is life in earth or air,
    And not with these at one?
            —*Written for "Cecil the Seer."*

IN THE WORLD OF CARE AND SORROW.

IN the world of care and sorrow
    Cloud and darkness veil the way,
But in heaven there waits a morrow
    Where the night shall turn to day,
Where the spirit-light in rising,
    Yet shall gild the clouds of fear,
And the shadows, long disguising,
    Lift and leave the landscape clear.

When the soul, amid that glory,
    Finds its earthly garments fall,
Harm and anguish end their story,
    Health and beauty come to all;
No more fleshly chains can fetter
    Faith that longs to soar above;
None to duty seems a debtor,
    And the only law is love.

There is ended earthly scheming,
    Earthly struggle sinks to sleep;
Souls have passed from deed to dreaming,
    And they have no watch to keep;

For the world has wrought its mission,
   And the wheels of labor rest;
And the faithful find fruition,
   And the true become the blest.
       —Written for "Cecil the Seer."

———

THE TRUMPETS CALL TO ACTION.

THE trumpets call to action
   Through all the threatened land,
No more is heard of faction,
   The time has come to band.
    What soul can see
The state in fear, and fail to be
Beneath the flag, enrolled with all
   That heed the trumpet's call?
    No patriots are they who can see
    The state in fear and fail to be
    Beneath the flag, enrolled with all
    That heed the trumpet's call.

The best of men are brothers.
   The worst can be a foe;
And not for self, but others,
   True men to battle go.
    No longer meek,
Where wrong is cruel, right is weak,

Or aught has brought the base to band,—
　They throng to lend a hand.
　　No true men are they who can see
　　The state in fear, and fail to be
　　Beneath the flag, enrolled with all
　　　That heed the trumpet's call.

Who, think you, live in story
　That live for self alone?
Who care to spread his glory
　That cares not for their own?
　　In every strife
That stirs the pulse to nobler life,
The man that has the thrilling heart,
He plays the thrilling part.
　　No heroes are they who can see
　　The state in fear, and fail to be
　　Beneath the flag, enrolled with all
　　　That heed the trumpet's call.

—Idem.

———

OH, WHY DO WE CARE?

OH, what is the matter, and why do we care
　For an empty, visionless whiff of air?
Ah, though the wind be nothing to see,
It bends and batters and breaks the tree;

And oh, we know a breeze that serves
To shock and shiver and shatter the nerves,
And snuff the light of life with a breath;
It has nothing to see, but it ends in death—
   Ho ho, ho ho,
    That blow, blow, blow, blow, blow!

Oh, what is the matter, and why do we care
For a silent sight of the sunshine there?
Ah, though no sound may rouse the ear,
The bud and blossom of spring are here;
And oh, we know a sight so bright
It cheers the world like heavenly light,
Till far away fly doubt and strife;
It has nothing to hear, but it lures to life—
   High high, high high,
    That eye, eye, eye, eye, eye!
          —Written for "The Ranch Girl."

AH, BOYS, WHEN WE FILL OUR GLASSES.

AH, boys, when we fill our glasses,
  We may drink to whatever else passes,
    But whenever we quaff
    To life's better half,
We must always drink to the lasses.

You may journey to Nice or to Paris
For a cough that a song may embarrass;
    But the air of the West
    Is the freshest and best;
And the sweetest, the air of its heiress.

                —Idem.

OUR LIVES ARE VAPORS.

OUR lives are vapors forced to roam,
    Of sun and storm the prey;
But cling like mists, with hills their home,
    Together while they may.

Chorus: And, friends, whate'er may come to you,
    Join hand and voice with mine,
And swear the love that here we knew
    Shall never know decline.

Our lives are vapors, whirled through skies,
    Where some by storms are torn,
And some the sunlight glorifies,
    And some to heaven are borne.

Chorus: But, friends, whate'er may come to
      you, etc.

Our lives are vapors wrecked and lost.
   None sail their journey through.
Ere long behind some blow that tost,
   Will naught be left but blue.

Chorus: But, friends, whate'er may come to
      you, etc.
      —Written for "The Ranch Girl."

——

MONEY AND MAN.

THE time will come when money
   Will pay what work is worth;
Will buy your task, and none will ask
   Your station or your birth.
The right to earnings will be won
By what a man himself has done.
          Oh!—
The time will come when money
   Will pay what work is worth.

The time will come when money
   Will not buy one a crown—
To lift a snob above the mob
   And keep all others down.

For men, to inward worth alert,
Will only bow to true desert.
                    Oh!—
The time will come when money
    Will not buy one a crown.

The time will come when money
    Will not seem more than man;
But hearts will yearn with all they earn
    To help all men they can.
In rolls of honor in that state,
Great love alone will make men great.
                         Oh!—
The time will come when money
    Will not seem more than man.
—*Written for "The Little Twin Tramps."*

JUST THE THING HE THINKS.

THE sun gives everything its light;
    The mind gives everything its thought;
And what we deem is dark or bright,
    Reflects but what ourselves have brought.
That friend, whose own extorting clinks
    In hands he holds to help the world;
That foe, from whom each neighbor shrinks

Though not returning blows he hurled,—
Is just the thing he thinks.

A college student with a bang,
  Who struts with open mouth about,
And thinks, by slinging slaps of slang,
  His tongue can lick all censure out;
Whose mouth, if busied not with drinks,
  When asked what he has learned at school,
Is kept as closed as if a sphynx,
  For fear to show himself a fool,—
Is just the thing he thinks.

A belle, made so by wiggling waist
  And tongue that never ceases wagging,
Who wanted once to wed in haste
  But long has found all lovers lagging,
And powders now, and paints and prinks,
  And stuffs the thin and straps the stout,
For fear, through ways that ape a minx,
  The world, alas, may find her out,—
Is just the thing she thinks.

A man who lost a former bride
  And mourns her memory on his hat,
A hat he gently waves aside
  That he may gaze more ladies at,

The while for each he dives yet shrinks
    For fear all love that he can vow
Behind that eye that winks and blinks
    Is hardly worth the having now,—
Is just the thing he thinks.

The man who boasts a family tree,
    And great grandpas that came and went,
Which proves to all, the more they see,
    How great has been his own descent;
And who from self-made people shrinks
    That now do what his grandpas did,
Lest other men may see the links
    That bind to what he wishes hid,—
Is just the thing he thinks.

The gallery-bird with flying sleeves
    That tempt us here to shoot or shoo;
The balcony-belle who half believes
    All music lures a beau to woo;
The dear bald head that nods and blinks;
    And each whose clapping bids us folks
Repeat our notes like bobolinks
    Lest some may think he miss'd our jokes,—
Is just the thing he thinks.

        —Written for "The Little Twin Tramps."

IT DOES NOT SEEM FREE TO ME.

OH you who prate of freedom,
 Say, are you fools or knaves?—
Of all the things men like the best,
 The first is being slaves.
Who ever yet bought coat or hat,
 Or wore a gown or bustle,
That dared defy the style in that
 Which made the parlor rustle?
Though it may clothe our dearest friend,
Outside our own set, in the end,
 The fashionless we hustle.
Oh, you may call that being free,
But it does not seem free to me.

Oh you who prate of freedom,
 You send your babes to schools,
And just when old enough to work,
 You turn them all to tools;
And they, lest when, left free from strife,
 Mere rest should bring them pleasure,
Are not content, till wedded life
 Is girt to slavery's measure;
Then, that more tyrants may be grown,
Each stocks a nursery of his own,
 And calls each sprout a treasure:—

Oh, you may call that being free,
But it does not seem free to me.

Oh you who prate of freedom,
   Work once was free for each.
But comes the boss—his voice is heard,
   And work is past your reach.
More cash you want.   Your savings go
   To pay another's bill.
And peace you want.   Before you know
   You vow, perchance, to kill.
You once had pay.   On freedom bent,
You serve a chief, nor get a cent,
   Who works you at his will:—
Oh, you may call that being free,
But it does not seem free to me.

Oh you who prate of freedom,
   In home, in state, in church,
If any realm could grant your wish,
   It would not end your search.
The place where most men like to be
   Is where with most they mingle;
And such a place none ever see
   So long as they keep single;
Nay, those, in all they care about,
Who always leave their neighbors out,
   Find life not worth this jingle:—

Oh, you may call that being free,
But it does not seem free to me.
—Written for "The Little Twin Tramps."

A FAIRY SONG.

TO-NIGHT, to-night, my fairies white,
The fair sweet air we sail.
But first a tune to tease the moon
That tempts us toward the vale:—
Who cares to go where roses glow
In sheen the moonlight sheds,
And globes of dew are sparkling through
The tent the spider spreads?
Your moonstruck fay may dance away
And crush the rose-leaves all to hay—
Who cares?—I don't!—Do you?

But note you there that maiden fair—
Ha, ha, a dainty bit!
She dreams a dream of love I deem.—
Queen Mab 's a wicked wit!
Come, come, a jump; and down we 'll thump;
And dance about her heart.
'T will beat and beat—aha, how sweet
The thrills we there shall start!

We 'll tickle her neck, and tickle her toes,
And tickle her little lips under her nose—
   Who cares?—I don't!—Do you?

And then we 'll huff that mourner gruff,
   Till he unknits his brow.
We 'll whiz and whiz about his phiz,
   And pinch his lips, I vow;
Then hide and seek in hair so sleek,
   And down each wrinkle spare;
And ply his eye, if dry, too dry;
   And slide the lashes there;
And when big drops begin to flow,
Oh, how we 'll dodge the flood, oh ho!—
   Who cares?—I don't!—Do you?

The moon may keep the earth asleep—
   We 'll twist things ere we go.
The beau shall toss a baby cross,
   The belle shall beat her beau;
The men be boys; and boys the toys
   Of girls that at them scream;
And when they wake, oh, how they 'll shake
   To find it all a dream!
They 'll think of wind and fly and flea;
But not of you, and not of me—
   Who cares?—I don't!—Do you?

       —Written for "A Life in Song," I.

LOVE AND TRUTH.

COME to the love that is coming now,
  Come from the world away;
Come to the source of joy, and bow,
  Bow to the sweetest sway.
Find but love for the heart that grieves,
Love for the work one never leaves,
Love for the worth that work achieves,
  Love; and woe will away.

Come to the truth that is coming now,
  Come from the world away;
Come to the source of right, and bow,
  Bow to the wisest sway.
Find in the way where all is light
Truth to impel the soul aright,
Truth to make all that awaits it bright,
  Truth; and doubt will away.

Come to love, and wherever you wend,
  All true life is begun.
Ever in bliss toward which you tend,
  Joy and the right are one.
Love—and the heart shall warmer glow;
Love—and the mind shall brighter grow;
Love with truth—and the soul shall go
  On to the lasting sun.

Come to the truth, and come as you may,
   All of love is begun.
Whether you feel or think your way,
   Love and the truth are one.
Love is the warmth, and truth the ray;
Truth is the light, and love the day;
Come to either, you wend your way
    Under the lasting sun.

                      —Idem.

THE WORLD THAT WHIRLS FOREVER.

SEE the world that whirls forever,
   Round and round and weary never,
Leaving sinning, glory winning
   Through its ever brightening way.
Oh, in worth the deeds of duty
Rival all the claims of beauty!
Onward world, with steadfast spinning,
   Learn to turn a perfect day.
    Work cannot go wrong for aye.
    Woes but roll to roll away.

World of faith, the years are dying
In which clouds about thee lying
Robe a wondrous waste of sighing,
   Empty throes of vain unrest.

Life, if right, whatever bearing,
Still for true success preparing,
Must outwit the wrong's ensnaring.
    Faith will find that faith is blest;
    Wrestle through its prayer for rest;
    Dwell with good a constant guest.

World of hope, the stars are o'er thee.
Dawn is waiting just before thee.
Heaven's own light, thy life invoking,
    Every promise bright reveals.
Fast shall rays that days are sending
Heaven and earth in one be blending;
Showing what the storm's dark cloaking,
    Tho' with rainbow belt, conceals.
    Night, too, blesses him who feels
    'T is a star in which he kneels.

World of love, the heavens above thee
Hold the clouds, and can but love thee.
Though in spring the storm sweep o'er thee,
    April's rain is autumn's gain.
Rock'd by wind and nursed by shower
Life will grow to leaf and flower;
Every harvesting before thee
    Shows the vintage is but rain
    Turn'd to wine the grapes obtain
    From the floods that fill the plain.

Onward world, desponding never,
Round and round, yet onward ever,
On where sense and sorrow sever,
   Onward move thy mission through.
Wisest deeds thy safety highten.
Wisest words thy thoughts enlighten.
Wisest views thy visions brighten.
   Holy wings thy way pursue.
   Heavenly outlines loom in view.
   Bliss is dawning down the blue.
               —Idem.

FATHER OF OUR SPIRITS, HEAR US.

FATHER of our spirits, hear us,
   And in mercy now draw near us,
And with Thy blest presence cheer us,
   While our spirits look to Thee.
Thou for whom the stars are burning,
Do not, Lord, disdain the yearning
Of the hearts to Thy heart turning,
   With their wants their only plea.

Long in doubt's dark ways abiding,
Lord, we need Thy light and guiding,
Minds to know, and souls confiding
   In Thy precious truth and love.

When Thine inward voice invited,
And desires for good incited,
We have still'd, because we slighted
　All that call'd our souls above.

Even if, forsaking pleasure,
We have sought for truth like treasure,
Oft we but would test the measure
　Of what our own strength could do;
And, beyond our best endeavor,
Full assurance found we never
That, if wrong, the old life ever
　Could be cancelled by the new.

Naught is left us, Lord, we feel it,
Holy writ and reason seal it,
And all loving lives reveal it,—
　But to cast ourselves on Thee.
Here we come before Thee kneeling,
Moved by far too little feeling;
Yet to grace divine appealing,
　Wilt Thou, Lord, reject our plea?

Nay, our souls for mercy sighing,
Think of Jesus, living, dying,
And they know Thy love replying
　Need not wait for worth in us.

With our strength impair'd and sinking,
From each nobler duty shrinking,
Lord, we praise Thee most in thinking
   Thou wilt yet receive us thus.

Thou wilt, Lord, from Thy high station,
Pardon us, and send salvation,
Till Thy Spirit's inspiration
   Make us all we ought to be.
Void of good, yet Thou canst make us
Fill'd with what Thou wilt. Oh, take us,
Own us, hold us, nor forsake us,
   For our spirits look to Thee.

               —*Idem., III.*

THE END.

THE AZTEC GOD, AND OTHER DRAMAS

By GEORGE L. RAYMOND

16MO, CLOTH EXTRA, $1.25

"The three dramas included in this volume represent a felicitous, intense, and melodious expression of art both from the artistic and poetic point of view. . . . Mr. Raymond's power is above all that of psychologist, and added thereto are the richest products of the imagination both in form and spirit. The book clearly discloses the work of a man possessed of an extremely refined critical poise, of a culture pure and classical, and a sensitive conception of what is sweetest and most ravishing in tone-quality. The most delicately perceptive ear could not detect a flaw in the mellow and rich music of the blank verse."—*Public Opinion*.

"It is not with the usual feeling of disappointment that one lays down this little book. One reads 'The Aztec God' with pleasure. . . . 'Cecil the Seer' is a drama of the occult. In it the author attempts to describe the conditions in the spiritual world exactly as they exist according to coinciding testimony of Swedenborg, of the modern Spiritualist, and of all supposed to have explored them in trance states. Indirectly, perhaps, the whole is a much needed satire upon the social, political, and religious conditions of our present materialistic life. . . . In 'Columbus' one finds a work which it is difficult to avoid injuring with fulsome praise. The character of the great discoverer is portrayed grandly and greatly. . . . It is difficult to conceive how anyone who cares for that which is best in literature . . . could fail to be strengthened and uplifted by this heroic treatment of one of the great stories of the world." —*N. Y. Press*.

"One must unreservedly commend the clear, vigorous statement, the rhythmic facility, the copious vocabulary, and the unvarying elevated tone of the three dramas. . . . The poetic quality reveals itself in breadth of vision and picturesque imagery. One is, indeed, not seldom in peril of forgetting plot and character-action in these dramas, because of the glowing imagination."—*Home Journal*.

"The time and place make the play an historic study of interest, aside from its undoubted high poetic quality and elevation of thought. . . . The metre of the dramas is Shakespearian, and that master's influence is constantly apparent. It is needless to say to those who know the author's remarkable abilities that the plays are substantial and reflect perfectly the author's mind."—*Portland Transcript*.

"The conquest of Mexico . . . has furnished the world with themes for wonder and romance. These Professor Raymond has brought into a thrilling story. . . . His studies in art and harmony give him a master's hand to paint the pictures that delineate the children of the sun." —*Dayton Journal*.

"The work is one of unusual power and brilliancy, and the thinker or the student of literature will find the book deserving of careful study."— *Toledo Blade*.

"A work of high poetic art, and worthy of the reputation of its accomplished author."—*N. Y. Observer*.

"Poetical compositions of an unusually high order both in the expression and in the dramatic conception."—*Denver Times*.

A LIFE IN SONG

By GEORGE L. RAYMOND

16MO, CLOTH EXTRA, $1.25

"An age-worn poet, dying amid strangers in a humble village home, leaves the record of his life in a pile of manuscript poems. These are claimed by a friend and comrade of the poet, but, at the request of the cottagers, he reads them over before taking them away. The poet's life is divided into seven books or 'notes,' because seven notes seem to make up the gamut of life. . . . This is the simple but unique plan, . . . which . . . forms but the mere outline of a remarkably fine study of the hopes, aspirations, and disappointments of life, . . . an American modern life. . . . The author sees poetry, and living poetry, where the most of men see prose. . . . The objection, so often brought against our young poets, that form outweighs the thought, cannot be urged in this instance, for the poems of Prof. Raymond are full of keen and searching comments upon life. Neither can the objection be urged of the lack of the human element. 'A Life in Song' is not only dramatic in tendency, but is singularly realistic and acute. . . . The volume will appeal to a large class of readers by reason of its clear, musical, flexible verse, its fine thought, and its intense human interest."—*Boston Transcript.*

"Professor Raymond is no dabbler in the problem of the human spirit, and no tyro in the art of word painting, as those who know his prose works can testify. These pages contain a mine of rich and disciplined reflection, and abound in beautiful passages."—*Hartford Theological Seminary Record.*

"Here are lines which, if printed in letters of gold upon the front of every pulpit, and practised by every one behind one, would transform the face of the theological world. . . . In short, if you are in search of ideas that are unconventional and up-to-date, get 'A Life in Song,' and read it."—*Unity.*

"Some day Dr. Raymond will be universally recognized as one of the leaders in the new thought-movement. . . . He is a poet in the truest sense. His ideals are ever of the highest, and his interpretation is of the clearest and sweetest. He has richness of genius, intensity of human feeling, and the refinement of culture. His lines are alive with action, luminous with thought and passion, and melodious with music."—*Cleveland World.*

"The main impulse and incident of the life are furnished by the enlistment of the hero in the anti-slavery cause. The story of his love is also a leading factor, and is beautifully told. The poem displays a mastery of poetic rhythm and construction, and, as a whole, is pervaded by the imaginative quality which lifts 'a life' into the region of poetry,—the peculiar quality which marks Wordsworth."—*Christian Intelligencer.*

"It is a great work, and shows that America has a great poet. . . . A century from now this poem will be known and quoted wherever fine thought is appreciated, or brave deeds sung."—*Western Rural.*

BALLADS AND OTHER POEMS

By GEORGE L. RAYMOND

16MO, CLOTH EXTRA, $1.25

"In the construction of the ballad, he has given some notable examples of what may be wrought of native material by one who has a tasteful ear and practised hand. If he does not come up to the standard of the ancient ballad, which is the model, he has done as well as any of the younger American authors who have attempted this kind of work, and there is true enjoyment in all that he has written. Of his other poems, the dramatic poem, 'Haydn,' is finished in form, and has literary value, as well as literary power."—*Boston Globe.*

"The author has achieved a very unusual success, a success to which genuine poetic power has not more contributed than wide reading and extensive preparation. The ballads overflow, not only with the general, but the very particular, truths of history."—*Cincinnati Times.*

"It may well find readers in abundance . . . for the sake of the many fine passages which it contains. . . . 'Ideals made Real' has one point of very high excellence . . . we have in the conception of the character of Edith the work of a genuinely dramatic poet. . . . In Edith we have a thoroughly masculine intellect in a thoroughly feminine soul, not merely by the author's assertion, but by actual exhibition. Every word that Edith speaks, every act that she does, is in accord with this conception. . . . It is sufficient, without doubt, to give life to a less worthy performance, and it proves beyond doubt that Mr. Raymond is the possessor of a poetic faculty which is worthy of the most careful and conscientious cultivation."—*N. Y. Evening Post.*

"A very thoughtful study of character . . . great knowledge of . . . aims and motives. . . . Such as read this poem will derive from it a benefit more lasting than the mere pleasure of the moment."—*London Spectator.*

"Mr. Raymond is a poet emphatically, and not a scribbler in rhyme.' *London Literary Churchman.*

"His is no mere utterance of dreams and fancies. His poetry takes hold on life; it enters the arena where its grandest and purest motives are discussed, and by the vigor and beauty of the language it holds itself on a level with the highest themes. . . . Every thoughtful reader . . . will wish that the poems had been longer or that there had been more of them. It would be possible to quote passage after passage of rare beauty."—*Utica Herald.*

" . . . Rhythmical in its flow and deliciously choice in language . . . indicating a deep acquaintance with human nature, while there is throughout a tone that speaks plainly of a high realization of the divine purpose in life . . . Not the least charming characteristic is its richness in pen-and-ink pictures marked by rare beauty and presenting irresistibly that which the poet saw in his mind's eye. . . . We confidently promise that any one taking it up will enjoy the reading throughout, that is, if there is any poetry in him."—*Boston Evening Journal.*